Outlaw in the Hills

Plays by Michael Wilcox
published by Methuen

Accounts
Lent
Massage and Other Plays
Rents
Green Fingers
Gay Plays Volumes One to Four (ed.)

Michael Wilcox

OUTLAW IN THE HILLS

A Writer's Year

Methuen

First published 1991
by Methuen London
Copyright © 1991 by Michael Wilcox

The author has asserted his moral rights

A CIP catalogue record for this book
is available from the British Library
ISBN 0 413 64910 5

Printed in Great Britain
by St Edmundsbury Press Ltd, Bury St Edmunds
and bound by Hunter & Foulis Ltd, Ebinburgh

List of Illustrations

1a My father, Denys Wilcox.
1b My family in 1951.
2a Aged fifteen.
2b C. P. Taylor.
3a Jean Anderson and Patience Collier in *Lent*, 1983.
3b The BBC television production of *Lent*, 1985.
4   Stevan Rimkus and Douglas Sannachan in *Rents*, 1984.
5a Dexter Fletcher as Rikki in *Massage*, 1986.
5b John Thaw, Kevin Whatley and Terence Hardiman in *Last Bus to Woodstock*, Central Television.
6   Penelope Walker as Milak in the WNO's production of *Tornrak*, 1990.
7   David Owen as Arthur with Penelope Walker in *Tornrak*.
8a The Haltwhistle Second XI in 1989.
8b A lucky bottom edge for four!

Acknowledgements and thanks for permission to reproduce photographs are due as follows: to Donald Cooper for plates 3a, 4 and 5a; to the BBC for plate 3b; to Zenith/Central Televison for plate 5b; to Clive Barda for plates 6 and 7.

1989

January

New Year's Eve and the roads are clear of snow! I've been down to Featherstone Castle for an evening meal with John Clark, the owner, his sister Susan and her family. There were twelve of us round the table, including a group of Oxford graduates who come to Featherstone around this time to run cross country.

Susan has been widowed for some years. Each of her four children, after doing well at university, has left home. Rachel is a Christian worker in the Sudan, Sarah works for Rank Hovis, Aidan is an expert on antique furniture and works for Phillips, the Fine Arts auctioneers, in Edinburgh. Crispin is a research scientist in America. Susan wants to enjoy the company of her children before they are scattered again.

John is staying in the Castle. He's seen the annual ritual of the blazing tar barrels at Allendale many times.

A few days earlier, a jumbo jet was blown up by a bomb. The fuselage crashed on to Lockerbie, a couple of minutes' flying time away, but many fragments of the aircraft were scattered over the Scottish Borders and north Northumberland. Hundreds of people were murdered.

The Wallace Arms is our local pub. It is about four miles south of Haltwhistle, the nearby town and shopping centre, which itself is on the A69 road that links Newcastle upon Tyne with Carlisle. In the nine years that I have lived in my present cottage, near

Kellah Farm, there have been three owners. The latest is David who moved up from the south some six months ago. He has never run a pub before. He doesn't say much and is slow about the place. There has been some talk about whether he'll last long, but he shows signs of settling in. On arrival, he had no idea how to play host to his guests and has lost trade as a result. We are all anxious that The Wallace Arms should stay open and not be sold again. It might become a private house, and we might lose our pub.

Our party moved from Featherstone Castle to The Wallace for an hour before driving over to Allendale, the two drivers dutifully abstaining from alcohol. A gang from the Young Farmers' Club was there. One of my first jobs of the New Year will be to write a half-hour play for them for production in February.

'Tell us about the play, then, Mike!' said Tom.

'Oh . . . right. Well I've got one idea.'

'You may as well tell us,' says Eli.

'I've promised not to dress you all up as animals. Right?'

'Right!'

They're fed up with being sheep.

'Well, there are these two lads. They're burglars. The court has imposed Community Service orders on them. They've been sent to work at this old castle and they have to set up the dining room for a banquet. One of them . . . he's dead cocky, and thinks he's going to get away with everything! The other lad just follows him about, like a sheep.'

'No sheep!' insists Tom.

'Hang on! Anyway, the fellow in charge of them, he says that when they've prepared the feast, they've got to pack and go. But they don't!'

'Is that it?' Margaret doesn't think that sounds much like a play.

'Not quite. They decide to hide behind the curtains and then all these ghosts . . . you know . . . phantoms . . . turn up for their annual dinner! The boys pretend to be waiters, but the game is given away when they can't walk through walls or closed doors like the others! So they're dragged in front of the chief ghost who says that unless the lads can entertain all his guests to everyone's satisfaction, they'll be beheaded at midnight!'

'Sounds quite good.'

'Do they get beheaded?'

'Well ... they do their best with Michael Jackson impersonations, juggling acts that they're no good at, and an attempt to perform an episode from *Dynasty*. There's a show of hands and the ghosts vote in favour of beheading the loud mouthed, cocky one!'

'That's the play?' says Tom, incredulously.

'Something like that!' I look at them to see what sort of response I'm getting. Bewilderment!

'Sounds OK. Plenty of parts,' says Eli helpfully.

'I think it's good,' says Angus. (Good old Angus!)

'You notice I said "lads" when I told you the story? Well, I think one should be a boy and the other a girl.'

'Are they evil ghosts?' asks Ian, the accordian player.

'No, not really. They were people like us. Neither good nor bad. Just the usual human mixture. They'd rather do good turns than evil ones, but can be a little wicked! They're all the people that have ever died in the castle. They meet up once a year, because when you're dead all the time it's fun to do something different occasionally.'

I'm glad to see the back of 1988. It has been a year full of disappointments and frustration. Since my spell on *Inspector Morse* (the Oxford based detective, played by John Thaw) in 1987, I have been working on two ninety-minute TV films. One commission came from BBC TV, London. Producer David Snodin and director Elijah Moshinski had seen my production of *Massage* at the Lyric Studio, Hammersmith, and had asked to see me about a film they had in mind. The result was that I started work on *Icons*, a black comedy set in the near future, about homophobia and Christian fundamentalism running riot in Britain. The basement of the National Gallery is turned into a studio for the mass production of neo-Victorian religious icons!

I told David Snodin from the outset that I didn't believe that the BBC would ever allow such a film to be made, but he encouraged me with his support. After four drafts, and just as the unusual storyline was showing signs of taking shape, David dumped the project. Six months' work was scrapped. I only received the initial part of the commissioning fee, so was left seriously out of pocket. Why does the BBC treat writers like this?

At Allendale, it is twenty to midnight. The market square and the streets leading to it are packed with people. A brass band has been warming up with popular tunes near the Church. Smoke starts to fill the night air as the thirty barrels are lit. To the sound of a drum (which reminds me of the search party in *Peter Grimes*) the procession starts its march round the streets of the town. All the bearers are well known characters from the area. Flames light up the sky, casting ghostly shadows over the hundreds of watching faces. Everyone fears that sooner or later, one of the flaming barrels will topple over, causing a disastrous accident.

During the procession, I meet a distant cousin of mine, Christopher Scales and his mother. I am astonished! I was told many years earlier that Christopher had been killed in a car accident! I conceal my surprise. In my mind, he has come back from the dead. We shake hands and I kiss his mother.

The other BBC TV commission of 1988 came from BBC Scotland, who had a great success with the Screen Two film of *Lent* that I wrote for them some years earlier. Producer Tom Kinninmont, who was also the producer of *Lent*, approached me about a new film. I came up with an idea about a Special Constable in the country, who turned from being a lay-about to becoming a born-again Law and Order fiend. Tom liked the idea and *Special* was the result.

After many months of work and five rewrites, tailored to suit the producer, Tom was enthusiastic. Then there was silence, and more silence, and no action, no production dates. *Special* seemed to have slipped into limbo. After a number of phonecalls, I got a return call from Tom saying that *Special* had been dropped. He blamed Bill Bryden, Head of TV Drama at BBC Scotland, for this and was most apologetic. Another six months of wasted work with little to show for it.

The experience of *Icons* and *Special* is not unusual. I was unlucky, but not especially so. Every playwright connected with TV drama has similar stories to tell. It is tempting to think that the commissioning producers are irresponsible, but the fault is not wholly theirs. They might well have proceeded with both films if the final decision had been left up to them, but the power of individual producers seems to have been curtailed in recent years. Part of the trouble is that the costs of making films for TV is far higher than the old video/studio jobs that used to be the fashion before Channel Four started its 'Film on Four' series of feature films. At the moment, co-production financing is the hot formula for seeing a project through to completion. The trouble is that odd ball films, like both of mine were becoming, don't fit.

The result of these two disasters is that I have been taken out of service for a year, when I could have been writing a new stage play, and I have nothing much to show for a lot of slog. That includes cash, which writers need like everyone else. Thank God for the money from *Inspector Morse*, which has seen me through! Playwrights approached by TV companies should remember that TV drama can seriously damage your brain and your cash flow. In each case mentioned, TV producers have approached me first, and not the other way round. They have persuaded me to accept a commission with the usual initial payment of about £3,000. But if you work for six or seven months, with no further installment of your fee, as happened with *Icons*, the writer's goodwill is eroded, to say the least.

The tar barrels have reached the bonfire at last. One by one they are hurled on and in an instant there is a tremendous roaring and crackling as the pinewood blazes upwards. Apostates, criminals, political undesirables, witches and homosexuals have been burnt to death in market squares like this one in previous centuries. I watch the ferocity of the flames with a mixture of awe and fear. Thousands of sparks are propelled high towards the stars in the intense heat and the crowd is forced back by the fire's anger.

There was a chance of a new stage play in 1988. I tried to get a commission from Peter James at the Lyric Hammersmith, where *Rents*, *Lent*, *78 Revolutions* and *Massage* have all been performed. I wanted to write a play for the main house rather than my familiar territory of the Studio. This is not because the larger auditorium is better in any artistic sense, but because of the scale of the play that I wanted to write.

The story is set in the middle of the last century. The Lord of a large Northumbrian estate, a widower, tries to woo an elderly lady who was his childhood passion and first love. She has returned to Northumberland after fifty years in India, where she has been married and brought up her family. Now her husband has died, she has returned to the North of England and her roots, only to discover the embers of the childhood romance still glowing. Running alongside this story is the mystery of the missing teenage son of one of his tenants. The old man turns detective in an attempt to uncover the secrets of his disappearance.

Peter James was interested, but wanted commercial management participation. Two weeks later I travelled down to London a second time, at the request of impresario Michael Codron. Michael had commissioned *Lent* some years earlier, but after lengthy consideration, decided that he did not wish to produce that play. *Lent* was dedicated to Michael Codron as a mark of respect for his interest in me.

I arrived at the Aldwych Theatre, where Michael's offices are situated, after my five-hour trip from Northumberland. Michael told me he didn't want to hear me talk about the play. Would I please write to him about it! The whole interview lasted about twelve minutes and achieved nothing that couldn't have been done by letter or by telephone. So after a night in London, I set off back north again, cursing my wasted time and the expense of it all.

In the event, Michael thought the story was rubbish. Peter James, to whom I presume, he also communicated this judgement, lost interest in the project very rapidly. I think it is a good story, and the power of first love, which is the link between the elderly romance and the missing boy, is well worth writing about. And sooner or later I am going to write the darned thing to prove it!

If I was a composer and not a playwright, would I have to go along to someone before being commissioned to write a symphony to hum and whistle the 'themes'? Of course not! If a writer is worth commissioning, why can't the people behind the commission just let the writer get on with it? I, like most writers, work best when I am writing out of my own compulsion, in my own way, about what interests me. That's how *Rents*, *Lent*, *Accounts* and *Massage* were written. How does trusty and much loved Peter James, or Michael Codron, know that my proposed play is not worth the tiny amount of money that they would need to invest? What can you tell about a play from a brief outline of the story? Not much! What matters is the subtlety with which the characters are drawn, the way the plot is developed and the craft with which the whole script is structured. And you can't pass judgement on any of that from an outline.

After fifteen years of continuous work as a playwright, with a reasonable track record, not to be trusted is profoundly depressing. It makes me angry and it saps my energy.

In the darkness, the crowd around the subsiding fire circulates in high spirits, wishing everyone a happy New Year. There is excitement and good will and even a little drunkenness. I meet David Sanderson and his lass. David is one of Allendale's fallen cherubs, and an ex-team-mate from my days with Allendale Cricket Club. He gives me an alcoholic hug and showers me with affectionate compliments, while his lass looks on with furrowed brow. He goes on about me being 'the best speaker', or something like that. I haven't a clue what he's talking about, but it doesn't much matter.

Eventually, I catch up with my Oxford friends and we find our way back to the cars.

'That's it! 1989!' says Susan with finality.

The mystery of young David Sanderson's 'best speaker' is solved! Steven Charlton, secretary of Allendale Cricket Club, has phoned to ask if I will be their guest speaker at their annual dinner. Of course, I am delighted to accept.

'You can bring a guest, if you want, Mike,' adds Stephen, who knows quite well that I live alone. 'And you get a free dinner!'

I spent a couple of years living near Allendale ten seasons ago. Before that I had a single room in a multiply-occupied house in Jesmond, Newcastle upon Tyne. In that single room, I had written my first plays. *Rents*, the play that first attracted national attention to my work, was written in that little room in which I slept, worked and lived my life.

'Rent boys' (young male prostitutes) may seem an odd choice of subject for a play. In fact, I was only one step away from the streets myself, my small room being the raft of normality to which I was clinging. During a two-week visit to Edinburgh in 1976, where I was giving a series of lectures at Queen Margaret College to earn money, I met a young man who, if not strictly speaking on the game, was not too far off it. He took me around the city, showing me the bars, the meeting places and gay haunts. He introduced me to all sorts of characters and was a wonderfully mischievous story-teller.

Each evening, I went back to my lodgings and wrote a short play, between two and five pages long, based on the experience of the day. This journalistic approach to script writing resulted in a group of related plays, to which I gave the collective title of *Rents*.

These were shown to fellow playwright and mentor, C. P. Taylor, who also lived in Northumberland. At that time, Cecil was artistic advisor to the Tyneside Theatre Company. He also had a close working relationship with the Traverse Theatre Company in Edinburgh. Cecil read my plays and thought they were promising. He advised me to send them to Chris Parr, who ran the Traverse Theatre. The result was that Chris, who is now a senior drama producer at BBC TV Pebble Mill, commissioned me to write a full length version of *Rents* based on the material that I had submitted. This was my big break, and *Rents* was eventually produced at the Traverse in 1979, with great success.

Before the production of *Rents*, which took place three years after its preliminary drafts, I was able to move from my single room in Newcastle to a rented cottage at Ninebanks, near Allendale, for £4.50 a week! I collected some basic furniture, and had a telephone installed. There were never any carpets down during my two-year stay in that happy place. I wrote a series of three plays for the Dovecot Arts Centre in Stockton on Tees, travelling over there once or twice a week, for which I earned my first regular income since becoming a playwright in 1974.

And that's when my interest in cricket started.

One morning, local farmer Martin Wallace, stopped at the door and asked if I'd ever played, but it didn't matter if I hadn't. Allendale Second team were short that afternoon and they'd rather send a full squad than be one short. I was delighted to be asked and soon found myself driving with my new team-mates over to Stamfordham. I managed to score twenty-one, including a straight six. The truth is, I'm a born slogger! I've always been a fast runner and good catcher, so I proved a useful fielder as well. My place in the Allendale Second team became a regular feature of Saturday afternoons!

There has always been a tradition of cricket in my family. George Wilcox founded Whitehaven Cricket Club in 1838! My father, Denys Wilcox, was captain of Essex, and my brother John played for Essex for a number of seasons. John's finest hour (in my estimation) was during a wonderful match in 1964, when Essex defeated the Australian Touring team. John scored forty-six not out in the first innings and fifty-three not out in the second, helping to win the match.

As a little boy, I hated the game. I was dragged off endlessly to watch my father, but preferred to sneak away and catch tadpoles and minnows instead. John, three years older than me, was the golden boy of the family and was eager to learn as much as he could about the game. Before his tenth birthday, John had a formidable technique and a prodigious array of strokes. My idea of net practice was to smash the ball as hard as I could over the bowler's head, which is where that straight six came from. There was, I suppose, jealousy of the treats and privileges afforded to my older brother. I wanted to do things he wasn't good at to develop my independence. For all that, we got on well enough and shared a bedroom right up to the eve of his wedding.

It came as no surprise one Christmas, when we were each given cowboy outfits, that John was presented with a Mounted Police uniform while I was cast as the Outlaw. So, indeed, it has remained. John is headmaster of Alleyn Court School, Westcliff-on-Sea, as were my father and grandfather, while I live on my wits in my hideout at the northern end of the Pennine Hills.

Tonight, I went to a meeting of the Haltwhistle Young Farmers' Club to discuss the play. There were about twenty people there, aged between twelve and twenty-five, with an equal mix of boys and girls. I repeated my *Ghosts' Banquet* story, and then mentioned that I had an alternative idea. This was set in the new born babies ward of a hospital. After the nurse has settled them all down for the night, the babies all start chatting about their experiences of being born and what their hopes were for the future!

This time, everyone was excited and I soon had a few pages of notes about all the different of babies that might be in the ward, including a cry baby, a mean baby, a greedy baby, a punk, a Hell's Angel, a lonely baby and a smelly baby! (Their ideas, not mine!) So I've been given a week to come up with a script for twenty or more actors, in which ten are to play different sorts of baby! And the rest? Well, we made a list of nursery rhymes and children's stories, including the inevitable *Postman Pat*. Maybe, the babies could be entertained by books that come to life? All that in a twenty-five-minute play! Wonderful!

I've written four or five such plays in the past. My first, in

1981, became the basis for *Accounts*, a play about a farming family that moves Northumberland to the Scottish Borders. This was the play that followed *Rents* at the Traverse Theatre. Peter Lichtenfels directed, and *Accounts* won the George Devine Award, which I shared that year with Hanif Kureishi, of *My Beautiful Laundrette* fame. After a successful run during the 1981 Edinburgh Festival, *Accounts* transferred to the Riverside Studios, Hammersmith, for a further ten performances. It has only received one other professional production, in the Dixon Studio of the Palace Theatre, Westcliff-on-Sea, where artistic director, Christopher Dunham, has been a loyal supporter of my plays for many years. The Dixon Studio provided the South East with an enterprising series of productions for a couple of seasons, but is now closed through lack of funds, to the delight of some of the local Conservatives.

As well as the new play for the Young Farmers, I have been asked to write for a new opera magazine, *Opera Now*, whose first issue is coming out in March. Antony Peattie is the commissioning editor. He used to work for the Welsh National Opera Company, for whom I am writing the libretto of a new opera called *Tornrak* with music by John Metcalf. I am really delighted to be asked. I have been a devoted collector of classical LPs, and now CDs, since I was a teenager.

Importantly, this journalistic work will provide me with a small income that I need urgently. In addition to the terminated BBC TV film commissions, the *Tornrak* opera libretto carries with it a meagre £1,000 fee! I will get a percentage of the box office, and if the opera is a success, I could do quite well out of it. But that is in the future, and I have bills to pay now. I have been offered £250 for each *Opera Now* article, and if Antony Peattie accepts one piece each month, that will cover my mortgage repayments and various household bills. What? For £250? Yes, indeed! Living in the country has many benefits, and relatively cheap housing is just one of them.

Other sources of income at present include both an American

sale of *Inspector Morse*, which I am told will be worth about £2,500, and a UK repeat, which should yield a little more.

I shall also be editing Volume Four of *Gay Plays* for Methuen, for the princely sum of £450. I am not aware of any forthcoming productions of any of my plays anywhere in the world. But the delightful thing in my business is that you never know what the next post, or the next phonecall, will bring. From the perspective of January, 1989 seems a very promising year, concluding, if my luck holds, with a performance of *Tornrak* in the Queen Elizabeth Hall on London's South Bank.

I have written the Young Farmers' play. It took a couple of days. It's a first draft, of course. That's not satisfactory, but they want a script straight away, and I have a whole lot of other things to write.

There was an encouraging turnout at the read through. I remember from my teaching days how sensitive some people are about being asked to read out loud. I explained that many professional actors are poor at reading a script, and that they are not expected to give a performance at a read through. The purpose is to give everyone an idea of what the thing is about, and, most importantly, to help me, the playwright. I don't yet know what it sounds like, so when they take parts and read it for the first few times, they are doing me an important favour.

They were so good natured about it all, and immediately volunteered for the many parts that I had written. They seemed to like the idea of being new born babies and there was laughter as the play unfolded for the first time. One or two read far too fast, as though there was some merit in speed. Others clearly found reading difficult, but the rest waited patiently while the reader stumbled through the speech. There is never a hint of meanness with these people. They want everyone to do their best and be happy.

At the end of the first reading, there seemed to be a general nod of approval. They all swapped parts for the second reading, and I even did some elementary 'blocking', so that the ten babies were set out in a neat row. We had a brief discussion about which order the babies should be in. There were lots of ideas. Meanwhile, John and Colin, who will be directing the play, were also studying the script for the first time. There won't be many rehearsals before the company travels to Hexham in February to perform the play, and I wanted everyone to have a clear idea of how I think the play works and what my various intentions were.

One of the babies, Lonely Boy, doesn't speak to anyone until the final part of the play:

LONELY BOY I want to tell you something.
HELL'S ANGEL It spoke!
PUNK I don't believe it!
PROFESSOR Ssshhh! Go on, Lonely Boy.
LONELY BOY I do have a name.
MEAN BABY Who cares?
OTHER BABIES We do!
LONELY BABY The nurse said I was 'orphan'.
SMELLY 'Orphan'?
PUNK He's got no parents.
MEAN BABY How was he born, then?
LONELY BOY I had a mother. For nine months she cursed me. She wanted to kill me. I fought her. Kicked her belly from the inside. Made her sick. Kept her awake at nights. I was trying to tell her . . . 'I'm alive. I'm a person. Stuck in your belly!' She never wanted me. Never loved me. She smoked. Drank herself silly. Took drugs. I thought . . . if I let her forget me for one second, I'm done for.
PUNK Poor Lonely Boy.
GREEDY You can't go back to her!
LONELY BOY When I was born, I shouted 'You bitch! I don't ever want to see you!' I kept my eyes tight shut when they cut me out of her. Like this! But she didn't want to see me either. The nurses . . . they washed me and wrapped me up. They put me in a bubble, then brought me in here.
GREEDY Didn't your mam even cuddle you a bit?

LONELY BOY No.

PUNK Have you ever been cuddled?

LONELY BOY The nurses have picked me up ... but that's not the same thing, is it?

HELL'S ANGEL My parents made a real fuss of me! I think we're going to get on great. I can't wait to have my first tattoo!

LONELY BOY I want to warn you ... and you ... and you! I'm born full of bitterness. I'm frightened. I don't know what it's going to lead to. When we're all grown up, if we make it that far, there's a good chance that it's going to be me that breaks into your house or attacks you in the park. I don't want that to happen. You've got to help me!

(from *Brats*)

Having set the thing in motion, I handed over to John and Colin, telling them that I'd come to the dress rehearsal if they wanted me to, and certainly to the performances. But from now on, it was over to them. I got my coat, said goodnight, and thank you to everyone, and left.

I longed to be a screen actor when I was a little boy. I was brought up at Westcliff-on-Sea, near Southend, about fifty miles east of London. I was only allowed to go to the cinema during the school holidays (we had no television until 1953, when I was ten years old). From a young age, I was allowed to go to any of the eighteen local cinemas on my own. So whilst my father was bedridden and dying upstairs, I would try and arrange to see as many films in the four-week holiday period as I could afford. My shilling a week pocket money would only let me see one film, ninepence being the going rate for a 'half', or under fourteen year old. So the trick was to persuade someone I knew to take me.

In *Lent*, the young Paul Blake, for whom I was the prototype, has a good friend in an old teacher, Mr Maitland, known as 'Matey' to the boys. Matey was based on Mr Herman, who lived in at Alleyn Court School, which was also my home. In real life, his nick-name was 'Hermy', and from the age of about six I was always banging on his door and begging him to take me to 'the pictures'. He often did. There were others on my hit list, whom I manipulated mercilessly.

My favourites were war and cowboy films. My brother John liked the Three Stooges, the Marx Brothers and Jerry Lewis. But I was knocked out by Joel McRae in *Buffalo Bill* and, at the age of eight, contrived to see it five times in a week at the Westcliff Metropole.

> PAUL *Buffalo Bill* was one of the best films I've ever seen. You saw his whole life, from when he was a boy like me, until he was practically dead. I liked it before he was famous. He had a friend who was an Indian, and he had to fight him to the death. That was sad. Then, at the end, he had a circus, and you knew what an exciting man he had been. But the people didn't care, and when he was old, with a white beard, he appeared in the circus ring for the last time. And he took off his hat to the crowd and the spotlights went off him one by one. And when the lights went on again, he wasn't there, and you knew that was the end of him and he was going to die. That bit made me cry. And when he killed his Indian friend. Matey thought it was good too. He always gives me treats in the holidays.
>
> (from *Lent*)

In later years, when I was sixteen, I think, I sneaked off to see *Serious Charge*, in which a decent and hearty clergyman was accused of undoing those things that he ought to have left done up of a boy at his Youth Club. Cliff Richard was one of the boys in the film, before he became a famous 'pop singer'. The theme of the film was distinctly hot in those days, and when Hermy and I bumped into each other in the ice cream queue, for he had also crept into the cinema (unknown to me), we were both embarrassed! We spoke an undertone greeting and returned to our respective, lonely seats.

My own experiences of 'indecent assault', or child abuse as it has come to be called, did not at the time seem to me to be so terrible. On one occasion, when I was eleven years old, three boys set upon me, holding me down on my back on the floor of a school dormitory. One of them started suffocating me by holding his hands over my nose and mouth, while he knelt on my arms. Another boy sat on my chest with his back to my face. The third pulled down my trousers and started playing with what had been, up to that moment, very private parts indeed. I was terrified of not being able to breathe and was on the verge of unconsciousness a couple of times. The odd thing was that all this was accompanied by abusive derision. 'Look! It's split!' meaning my arse. 'Roundhead! Roundhead!' referring to my circumcised penis. The boy sitting on my chest spat on my balls. The other played with me roughly and stuck his finger into my anus. Then, mission accomplished, they all ran off! I think their intention, spurred on by devilment, had been humiliation, rather than rape. Or initiation, perhaps? I was frightened and upset, and I cried. Later, we all played marbles and football together, as though nothing had happened. The boy who had handled me so roughly even gave me some highly prized cheese labels (a craze at the time) for my collection!

Shortly afterwards, I was assaulted on the London Underground. I was travelling to Farnham in Surrey to stay with my Aunt Hilda, and, with my fishing rod and suitcase, was finding my way from Tower Hill to Waterloo. As usual, I was on my own. I don't recall anyone ever mentioning that it might be unwise for an eleven-year-old to travel without an adult and I preferred to look after myself.

In a crowded train, with all the seats taken and people squashed together, I felt a hand start to play with my balls through my flannel shorts. There were so many people around me that I was not sure at first who was taking such a liberty. I went very red in the face before I realised that it was a pin-striped City gent, with a leather briefcase, who was looking totally unconcerned in another direction so he didn't give the game away! Feeling guilty myself, I turned round so that he would have to stop what he was doing, while the train rumbled on. Presented now with my bottom, he continued his fondling with unabated enthusiasm, much to my surprise and continued embarrassment.

Then the train arrived in a station, there were people getting off and on, and we all got shifted around. That was the end of it. I glanced angrily at the man, who took not the blindest notice of me, and I thought what a rotten lot adults were, and that men who looked posh and professional were the worst of all! A wise observation that has been reinforced many times since.

My third instance of child abuse is far more serious. I was a victim of ignorance. As I tried my best to grow up, the adults around me found it quite impossible to discuss or explain what were mysteriously referred to as 'the facts of life'.

Like Paul Blake in *Lent*, my best endeavours only confused the issue. So I grew up knowing nothing of orgasms or how humans were conceived. I knew women got pregnant, but had no idea how. Why anyone should have imagined that this state of affairs was beneficial to us youngsters is hard to explain. Notions of innocence and purity were compounded together in a wicked crucible with guilt, fear, and a Victorian fundamentalist interpretation of the Bible.

> PAUL Sir... you know Mr Edwards talks to the boys when they leave... you know... the leavers' talk... well... what does he say?
>
> MATEY How should I know?
>
> PAUL You do know! I'm sure you do!
>
> MATEY He gives them all an old boys' tie.
>
> PAUL There's more to it than that, sir.
>
> MATEY He shakes hands and wishes them good luck at their public schools... and tells them not to let the side down.
>
> PAUL Why won't anyone tell me? I know it's about the facts of life. I feel stupid not knowing about things. Nobody tells you anything at this school.
>
> MATEY I doubt very much whether Edwards is an authority on the facts of life, dear boy. When I was a boy, we learnt such things in the dormitory at nights.

PAUL Did you? Did you, Matey?
MATEY Well . . . I mean . . . not exactly . . . some things . . .
PAUL I have learnt some things. Some quite dirty things. But I still don't understand. I can't make sense of it all. I don't like growing up. I've been perfectly happy the way I am. I don't want to grow up. I think hair on your body is ugly. Trevis used to be quite nice, but he's become hairy . . . you know . . . round his thing . . . I don't like him any more. I don't want to change. Why do things keep happening to you that spoil everything?
MATEY Oh God! let's talk about cricket.

(from *Lent*)

I was not alone. The attack by those three boys, who were at other times my friends, was an act of desperation to discover more, rather than an attempt to satisfy lust. I'm sure lust had nothing to do with it.

Like Paul Blake in *Lent*, I also shaved off my first pubic hairs with my dead father's razor. If no one would explain what was happening to me in a way that made any sense, anything I could do to preserve my former state seemed like a good idea.

I was conscious of sexual stimulation and excitement at a very early age, but had no explanation for it. I started having all the sensations associated with nocturnal orgasms from the age of about seven, although no semen was actually produced. When I mentioned what had happened at breakfast, my mother looked in a worried fashion at my father.

'He can't be . . . he's too young,' she said.

'Just a silly dream,' said my father.

Silly dream?

I had entered into the garden of Beauty and the Beast, as illustrated in Arthur Mee's children's encyclopaedia! The Beast in the picture had a boar's head, with wicked tusks protruding from its mouth. In my dream, I replaced the maiden and was in the arms of the Beast, who became like an angel in my embrace. This led to an ecstatic sensation, in my unexplored groin, of the most burning and intense orgasm. I awoke with a cry, and could only bring the incandescence (Victorian lingo was all I had to explain things) to an end by clutching myself and thrashing about on my bed.

I think I deserved a better explanation than 'a silly dream'! This experience was repeated a few times before I became a teenager, and was a clear indication of what lay ahead. It also occurred before the other experiences already mentioned. The homoerotic nature of my dreaming came from within me and was a part of me from birth. No doubt about that.

Antony Peattie has phoned to say that he likes my first article for *Opera Now* magazine. It was called 'Recording the Drama' and was about the ways different producers of opera recordings have attempted to provide a theatrical experience in the recording studio.

Antony says that he'd like something for the April issue and that there's a deadline of 11 February for contributions. The April edition is full of arcane material, he says, so I suggest it needs a little 'home cooking'. How about an extended version of my piece about *Tosca*, that I wrote for the Welsh National Opera Newsletter last year? Antony thinks that's a great idea! Good! To work at once!

There were plenty of whispers about what Mr Noble, our headmaster, would say to us thirteen-year-olds at 'the leavers' talk'. Presumably, 'the facts of life' would be revealed in glorious technicolour. No such luck!

We assembled, full of expectation, in the gymnasium at break time. Mr Noble arrived, consumed with embarrassment, and we all stood in a state of suppressed excitement beneath a rickety basketball net.

'It's my duty ... a headmaster's duty ... to talk to you before you pass on ... I mean ... to your Public Schools. I know you're not ready for this. Anyway ... the seed is ripening within you!'

It is?

'You will soon be coming to that sort of age, at least. And it's not a good idea to summon up the seed. You know ... in dark corners ... together. It's a bad habit. You might enjoy it. And that's not a good thing. So don't do it, will you.'

Don't do what, for God's sake? Summon up the seed? What the hell's he talking about?

'Well! That's got that over! Now here are your old boy ties. Good luck! Come back and see us some time.'

'That man's a complete idiot!' whispered Hooper on our way out of the gym. How true! Well said! I was fond of Hooper.

Since 1979, I have been a client of the International Copyright Bureau in Charing Cross Road, London. For my first five years of being a playwright, I managed all my own affairs, trying to sell my work and sorting out the terms of contracts, which generally meant accepting whatever I was offered.

After *Rents* had raised a few eyebrows at the Edinburgh Festival that year, impresario Peter Bridge (who was making a comeback after some years of absence from the West End with a revival of J. B. Priestley's 1932 hit, *Dangerous Corner*) was determined to bring my play to London. Peter insisted, quite rightly, that I should have an agent.

'I know just the person! Margery Vosper! I'll take you to meet her. If you don't think she's right, I'll find someone else. She might not like you, of course.'

The truth was that both Peter and Margery Vosper were far from well. Each had had their day. Margery cast a fierce eye over me after reading *Rents*, which, I learnt, had amused her greatly.

'You made me laugh,' she said grimly. 'You must be good.'

Peter Bridge, of course, had known her for decades, and he was clearly looking forward to reviving old times. I thought it was fun too, and Margery, who ran the International Copyright Bureau, became my agent.

I suppose the sensible advice to any playwright seeking an agent is to look for someone who, with a bit of luck, you can work with for the next twenty-five years. I knew that but I liked being swept along by events and was instantly fond of both Peter and Margery.

This story doesn't have a happy ending. Peter Bridge tried his best to find a West End theatre for *Rents*, but failed. He was convinced he would get the Ambassadors Theatre, which was the perfect size and a beautiful house. But when the manager, Mr Jay, read my play, he found it too shocking for words.

However saturated the commercial theatre may be with homosexuals, only the most discreet, closeted of plays with homosexual themes are generally allowed in. Peter Bridge pulled off a coup many years earlier when he got *Boys in the Band* through the back door. I doubt if Martin Sherman's classic play *Bent* would have lasted in the West End without Ian McKellen's support, not because there wasn't an appreciative audience for it, but because of the subject matter. More recently, *The Normal Heart* and *Torch Song Trilogy* managed to break the unwritten embargo for a while. But the truth is that the commercial theatre in Britain is profoundly homophobic.

The subsidised theatre isn't much better. Now, with the notorious 'section 28', which makes it an offence for a Local Authority to 'promote homosexuality', and with so many committees packed with homophobic Tories, the subsidised theatre companies are wary of placing their funding in jeopardy with any sort of controversial production.

So *Rents*, first written in 1976, and eventually performed in 1979, was effectively removed from the scene until Peter Bridge's rights in the play were exhausted. In that time, poor Margery Vosper died, and the International Copyright Bureau seemed, from my point of view, to be in a state of confusion. Later, the firm was taken over by Joy Westendarp, who has done a splendid job reviving its fortunes. She has become a great personal friend and counsellor in the process.

Peter Bridge lived long enough to see *Rents* in production at the Lyric, Hammersmith, where it was presented in a new production in 1981. It was an immediate box office success. The critics mostly gave the play a cautious nod of approval.

Since then, *Rents* has had a successful commercial tour of Australia, and a brief run in San Francisco. But it never made it into the West End, and I doubt if it ever will now.

Peter Bridge phoned me a few days before he died.

'Michael! Don't say a thing! Just listen, dear boy. I've cost you a fortune! A fortune! I'm so sorry.'

'Doesn't matter, Peter . . .'

'No! Don't interrupt! Stick at it! You're going to do terribly well. I know about these things. I love you very much. Goodbye, my dear . . .'

There has been a great domestic drama at The Wallace Arms.

I have been in the habit of going there from about six o'clock till seven-fifteen, and having a couple of pints while my supper is cooking at home. There are only two or three regulars at this time, including David Bean, novelist, broadcaster and playwright.

Last evening, I was chattering away a little more than usual, but after ten years, we have grown tolerant of each other's more tedious moments. David, the new publican, was prowling round the bar in his accustomed, silent way, looking as though he resented the intrusion of customers into his life. Someone started to talk about the effects of moving from the city into the country, since all of the four or five people present had done just that.

'Take David, here,' I blurted out, meaning David the publican, 'When he came up here a few months ago, he looked tired out . . . and a misery . . . and grey! Now he's full of vigour! There's colour in his cheeks and he looks ten years younger! Don't you, David!'

There was a moment's silence.

'Get out!' said David.

I thought he was joking! Everyone looked embarrassed.

'Go on! Get out!' he repeated.

I looked at him in astonishment. He grabbed my glass and emptied the beer into the sink.

'David,' I said quietly, 'Are you serious?'

He lowered his face so that it was a few inches away from where I was sitting.

'Look at my face . . . and then you'll see I'm serious!'

I looked into his face to see what was there. It was not the face of an angry man. That interested me. It was the face of someone who was enjoying this unpleasantness. There was a deathly hush in the bar.

'I can see from your face that you do indeed mean it, David. Would you like a moment to reconsider this?'

'No I wouldn't! Leave now!'

I was evidently wrong about the beneficial effect of country air.

I determined to retain some dignity in this wretched situation. I believe the others present were caught quite off balance, as I had been myself, and they kept silent.

'Right!' I said, getting off the bar stool. 'Goodnight everybody!'

'Goodnight, Michael!' they all said supportively.

So I went home to my supper.

Why would a man behave like this? The offending remark was, at worst, marginally cheeky. I knew from the lack of anger in his face that David had been waiting for an opportunity to throw me out. He was not acting on the spur of the moment. Homophobia? A bit of queer bashing? I'm not convinced, but it is possible. I had given him no rational reason for barring me.

Since news travels fast in the country, and people have very long memories, he'll have to live with his follies like the rest of us.

As for me, I really am one of the outlaws now.

February

I'd better admit now to one especial vanity. I want to appear in a film in which there is a cricket match! When I was a boy, I would have settled for riding into battle with Alexander the Great, or being captured by Apaches and brought up as a brave. But I've grown up and I want to be in a cricket match movie.

I nearly made it some years ago when I wrote a poor script for the BBC called *Cricket*, which far too many people remember, to my continued embarrassment. I got all togged up and even made it out to the crease, but for some reason, my friend, director

Michael Darlow, kept me continuously away from facing the bowling! I was, of course, itching to have my straight six recorded for all to marvel at, but it was not to be. Michael reckoned he had got all the footage he needed, and I was dispatched to the pavilion to make way for actor Jeremy Child, who proceeded to thump the ball all over the ground!

Somewhere on the BBC editing floor there is an out-take of me turning round halfway off the field and shouting at the director, 'That's the last time you direct a film of mine, Darlow!' Michael, of course, later directed *Accounts* for Film on Four, with great success and distinction.

Not to be thwarted, I have paid the special introductory price of £30 to have myself included on the new computerised 'Lasercast' system. Using my Equity name of Denys Wilcox, I have filled in my form in such a way that any director looking for cricketers for a match sequence will be fed my name by the casting computer! Since I have absolutely no ambitions as an actor, I have made sure that only an imbecilic producer would engage me to do anything other than play cricket, squash or tennis, or ride a racing bicycle!

Usually, the sporting scenes in films are laughably unconvincing. This is partly because the people taking part aren't much good at what they are supposed to be doing (that Australian *Bodyline* TV drama was a joke, especially the bowling sequences, which were, after all, at the centre of the controversy!) and partly because there is so much professional sport on the television that we know what the real thing looks like.

Anyway, here I am, ready to make my debut in front of the camera, if anyone wants me!

This month has started with my first trip of the year to London. My agent, Joy, was contacted by Software Production Enterprises, who specialise in technology videos. Their manager, Norman Burrows, was looking for a writer to work on a project for the British Medical Association. For some reason, they contacted me.

I met Norman Burrows in the company's Soho offices and have

found myself involved in an interesting twenty-five-minute drama about a heroin addict (female, early twenties) who visits a doctor (male, late forties) in his surgery. They have never met before. She is desperate for a fix. He is unused to treating addicts. What does he do?

The play will be shown to doctors, and will be bundled with legal and ethical advice intended to inform post viewing discussion. Only the script of the drama is my responsibility. For this I am expected to receive no payment! The BMA fund such films from charitable donations, and I am told that nobody connected with the production is paid any fee. If that is the case, then I am prepared to accept the situation, although I don't doubt that if I ever needed specialist medical advice, it would cost the earth. Oh yes – the script is wanted by next week!

I have access to a flat in London whenever I need it. Geraldine Easter runs a film company called The Filmworks from a house in Hammersmith. I have a key and am made welcome whenever I am in town. One of the most heartening legacies from my association with the Lyric Theatre, Hammersmith, has been the small group of loyal and generous friends who have shown me every support. It's a case of 'Michael lives with Geraldine and Tony'! Tony is about to leave his job with BBC Enterprises to become Director of Sales for Central Television.

Geraldine Easter produced the highly successful documentary *In the Footsteps of Scott* in which an intrepid band of explorers managed to walk to the South Pole! Her latest enterprise is equally dotty. At the end of my visit, I was up at dawn to see her off to China, where she is in search of the 'Wild Man', the Chinese Yeti! Knowing Geraldine, she'll find the damned thing, turn anthropology on its head, and find herself at war with millions of evolutionary fundamentalists.

Finding a Gents' toilet in the BMA's magnificent HQ building would baffle a professional treasure hunter. I've come to the conclusion that doctors only use glass jars.

Dr John Dawson, who is responsible for my drug addiction script at the BMA, gave me a further briefing about the project. He clarified the 'hidden agenda' of the play. He feared that too many GPs were unwilling to treat addicts, partly out of moral distaste, and partly out of fear and ignorance of AIDS.

This admission from a senior BMA official is alarming. Part of the purpose of the script is to show where the responsibility of GPs actually lies, and how they might treat a patient at the first encounter. John Dawson wanted the script to have a heterosexual context, partly to counteract all the publicity that has suggested, mischievously, that AIDS is a homosexual problem, but also because a homosexual patient would further alienate the mass of GPs, whom he considered homophobic.

Considering that one in a hundred males between the ages of fifteen and thirty-five in the Edinburgh region is thought to be HIV positive now, with the scale of infection rising constantly (Dawson's figures), the medical profession would appear to be in a state of crisis over the moral and ethical implications of drug addiction and AIDS.

What is clear to me is that the present situation redefines morality. A readily available supply of sterile needles is essential without further delay, nationwide and in all institutions, including prisons.

That such obvious and pragmatic action should be resisted by both Thatcher's Conservative Government and a substantial medical lobby within the BMA itself, Dr John Dawson not withstanding, raises the question of whether there is not a 'hidden agenda' on the extreme political right, namely that a population 'cull' of addicts, criminals, homosexuals and the sexually promiscuous is a good way of purifying the nation!

Anyone with such evil beliefs would no doubt have been heartened by pronouncements from junior Minister Douglas Hogg, who, on a recent BBC *Panorama* programme, refused to admit that there was a drugs or AIDS problem in prisons, and ruled out absolutely the possibility of supplying prisoners with sterile needles or condoms.

Much more jolly was my lunch with *Opera Now* magazine's Antony Peattie, cuddly, with a sharp eye. We conspired like a couple of truants, swapping gossip, and planning juicy articles.

I usually arrange to meet my London lunch dates in Brief Encounter, a gay bar next to the English National Opera's Coliseum. I prefer Brief Encounter partly because it is easy to find and near lots of restaurants, expensive and cheap, and partly because I dislike most straight pubs so much. Why? In straight pubs, the emphasis seems to be on drinking, rather than company; on aggression and macho exclusivity, rather than gentle curiosity in one's neighbour. In a gay bar it is unusual to see anyone drinking fast or in unsocial quantities. The atmosphere tends to combine a streetwise worldliness with friendly, or sometimes raunchy, good humour.

On this occasion, the upstairs bar was being refurbished and only the basement was open. It was airless and smelt musty (to put it politely), which dented my appreciation of the place. But tackiness is not without its own appeal. A beautiful young barman greeted all his customers as though he was pleased they had come, transforming, through his own personality, a dingy cellar into a palace.

After lunch, Antony took me back to the *Opera Now* offices and introduced me to the editor, warm and friendly Mel Cooper. They were all buzzing with appointments to keep, and Mel asked me back the following day.

I have always wanted a life's companion. Someone to share things with. Someone to go home to. Someone who comes home to me. I say 'companion' rather than 'lover' not out of prudery, but because that is exactly what I mean. Lovers are easily found. Sexual encounters, of the now necessarily safe variety, are easily achieved. But a true companion is elusive indeed.

I blame myself for this. I balance my own, intense, egocentricity with erratic bouts of generosity. I hold people at bay, frightening them off with solitary moodiness. 'I'm working. Can I get back to you in a few days?' 'Look! I need to be alone. I can't work with anyone else in the house.' 'I've got to do another draft by the last post on Thursday. I'll call you at the weekend. No! Hang on! I'm playing cricket on Saturday. Oh . . . and on Sunday. Do you like cricket?' And so on.

The trouble is, it's all true! It is difficult to work when there's a visitor staying. I'm not used to having anyone in the house. I know he's there, even if he's not in the room. And writers find any excuse for not working. Who wouldn't rather spend the day walking in the Lake District (an hour's drive from my house), or walk Hadrian's Wall (ten minutes away), or walk along the South Tyne, spying on fish, birds, red squirrels, foxes, wild deer, with the Pennine Hills beyond? A visitor means holiday time!

I've turned living alone into a fine art. I sleep from after midnight to six o'clock. Listen to the news, make tea, then work till lunchtime. After that I leave the house, making trips to Newcastle or Carlisle, where I stalk the record and book shops, hunting down bargains. Once a week, I go to the municipal sauna for a couple of hours. Then it's back home again (an hour's drive) and I cook, watch television and listen to music.

In the summer, I'm involved with Haltwhistle Cricket Club two or three times a week. This year, I'm captain of the Second XI, which I am looking forward to greatly. Then there are other local matches at Featherstone Castle. In my solitary state, I am never unoccupied.

But I am lonely. I resent my isolation, as though it was something someone else has done to me, and not my own responsibility.

Since my banning from The Wallace Arms, I have not searched further afield for somewhere to drink. My old habit did not extend beyond ten pints of beer a week, but my main purpose for going had been a social rather than alcoholic imperative. Nor am I in the habit of keeping booze in the house, unless I am entertaining visitors. So, in effect, I am in the process of completely drying out! Expect a full report on the effects of this drastic state of affairs later.

More interesting has been the response of others to what happened. Every shop I go into in Haltwhistle has some merry quip about me and The Wallace. Young Shaun Smith in Billy Bell's, the fish merchant, who up till now has been very quiet and shy, greeted me with uncontrollable mirth.

'What happened, like?'

'Not much.'

'But you've always struck me as such a quiet sort of a fellow,' Shaun tells me as he hands over half a dozen large eggs and a Cumberland pie. 'I think it's hilarious, as a matter of fact!'

'Bona' Hepple at Haltwhistle squash club, who is destined (I trust) to be one of the star bowlers of the Second team this summer, wanted a blow by blow account of what happened.

'I think that's terrible,' he said in his slow, considered way, as though the millenium had come.

Margaret Morrelee, secretary of the Young Farmers, phoned up. 'Ridiculous! That man has quite the wrong attitude! The other night he told us to stop singing and get down off the tables! It's getting hopeless there! Honestly!'

I note, however, that most of the regulars, who have escaped dismissal so far, keep going there. The real ale is good. It is clear where priorities lie.

Mr Unsworth refused to teach Latin after lunch. He said afternoons were better for stories. To my eight-year-old sensibilities, this concession should have been extended to mornings as well. He spent a whole term reading *Don Quixote* from the Penguin translation. He knew the text thoroughly, and selected lengthy extracts, filling in the intervening narrative himself.

We laughed, were astonished, let out cries of disbelief at the Don's antics, and tried to conceal our tears at his death.

Then Mr Unsworth read us *The Song of Roland*, the medieval French romance, the great love affair of Roland and Oliver, the shepherd boy and the young knight from the court of Charlemagne. This, I knew from the first page, was my story! The two boys swore life-long loyalty. They exchanged gifts. There was a social, class barrier between them, one being a commoner and the other nobly born. I managed to identify with both at once.

They had wonderful adventures. Unknown to each other, they were champions of rival armies, sent out before the other men to fight to the death. After many hours of wearisome combat, one lost his helmet, thus revealing his identity to the other. Instead of fighting on, they fell into each other's arms, to the astonishment of both armies. Love and Peace won the day.

But at the last and most dreadful battle, there was a fatal delay in sounding the horn that would have summoned reinforcements from the next valley. Mortally wounded, Roland (or was it Oliver?) raised the horn to his lips and sounded a note that echoed round the hills like a requiem, before dying in the arms of his friend.

Wasn't that the greatest story ever told to an eight-year-old? How could people think of Latin and Mathematics and spelling tests when there were such tales to tell?

And how inspired of our teacher to enthrall us with classics of European literature, and how unusual in 1951. I have, I should add, forgotten every detail of every Latin lesson he ever taught us.

I took the train to Edinburgh and a taxi from Waverley Station to the Muirhouse Health Clinic. The taxi driver gave me a second look when I told him where I wanted to go, as though I was asking him to ferry me across the waters of Lethe.

Dr Roy Robertson (doctors are joining soldiers and policemen in looking younger every day) greeted me in his surgery. I was shown to his chair while he sat half-sprawled on the examination couch. He confirmed that one per cent of males between fifteen and thirty-five in the Lothian region were indeed HIV positive.

'Is this percentage increasing steadily?'

'We suspect that is the case.'

'And at what point do you expect things to level out?'

'Ummmm... impossible to say.'

He told me various stories about his work. I noted down the crucial, factual information that a playwright needs. What drugs might my fictional addict have tried? (Substantial list. I guess at the spellings.) Would the doctor conduct a full body examination on her first visit? (Only if the patient was complaining of specific body pains.) Would he give her methodone? (No. Not on a first consultation. If she has survived for five years on her wits, she can get by for a few more days while the doctor finds out more about her previous medical history.) Free sterile needles? (Yes, preferably on a one-for-one swap with a dirty needle.) Free condoms? (Yes.) How many? (Two packets.)

There is a MASH-like jollity about the place. Everyone goes around smiling blissfully, being good-natured to a fault and making jokes. '... he's dying of AIDS, as a matter of fact,' Roy Robertson adds, casually, to an anonymous case history. The truth is that most of his patients will die as a result of AIDS, sooner or later. But this is spoken of with the emotional cut-off of the professional. What private griefs have to be contained, I can only guess at, but somewhere, sometime, there must be a personal price to pay for such closeting of human tragedy.

Writing a play requires the playwright not to make technical errors. The doctors watching the finished drama need to be convinced at the authenticity of what they're seeing. That's not the same as the playwright knowing enough to write a text book on the subject.

After forty-five minutes, I was back in a taxi with two pages of crucial notes, heading for Waverley Station once more.

The following day, I completed the first draft of the twenty-five-minute screenplay in six hours.

DR MCHENRY You suggested earlier that you were going on the streets tonight.
MRS WEST Yes.
MCHENRY For money?
WEST If...

MCHENRY Yes?
WEST If you gave me methodone I wouldn't have to.
MCHENRY I have no intention of giving you methodone on a first interview, Mrs West.
WEST Then you don't give me much choice, do you?
MCHENRY Choice? You have a choice. You can choose not to sell yourself for sex. You can choose not to risk infecting others with HIV.
WEST I need to get a fix somehow. It's not my fault!
MCHENRY You decided to inject yourself . . .
WEST That was years ago! I need help now!
MCHENRY . . . in the first instance, you did!
WEST (*on the offensive*) I didn't know about HIV five years ago! I didn't know about AIDS then! You did! You knew about AIDS and you didn't warn us! Why not? What were you doing five years ago, doctor? I AM your responsibility!

(from *Next?*)

After two days of listening to various performances of Gershwin's *Porgy and Bess* in preparation for an *Opera Now* review of Simon Rattle's new recording, I was up before dawn to travel to Aberystwyth, where my 1986 play *Massage* is on the modern drama syllabus. The journey involved changing trains at Crewe and Shrewsbury and, true to form, British Rail was running late enough for me to miss one connection, and leave me, and scores of other passengers stranded for ages on a miserable, single track line in central Wales.

But how wonderful to be met by lecturer, Ian Lucas, at the station, and to be whisked off to a splendid boarding house on the windswept Promenade. With spray from the sea whistling round our ears, Ian showed me where I was going to spend the next couple of nights.

'I've always wanted to stay in a place like this,' I said wearily. Ian laughed.

But I meant it!

Alleyn Court School was started by my grandfather in 1904 at Westcliff-on-Sea on the Essex side of the Thames Estuary. The buildings were requisitioned by the army at the outbreak of the Second World War and the school moved to a country house in Devonshire. That's where I was born in 1943.

I was four years old when we all moved back to the original school at Westcliff-on-Sea. I remember the rail journey and being told to look out for the white horse, carved in chalk on an adjacent hillside. The idea of a giant horse, as white as snow, galloping across the hills as the train steamed past, seemed wonderfully exciting. The images in my imagination far outstripped the disappointing glimpse we had of it.

But Westcliff, with its sea front leading to the colourful resort of Southend-on-Sea and its interminable pier, was full of new adventures. Day-trippers from the East End of London always seemed to be having tremendous fun that I wanted to be part of.

There were Punch and Judy shows on the beach, frightening and fascinating. The trick was to run like mad when they came round with the hat to collect our pennies. To this day, I'm not sure how the story ends.

There were the side shows, Rossi's Ice Cream and ancient penny in the slot machines. Pennies were pennies in those days. Big, heavy coins that wore holes in your short trouser pockets and clinked impressively when fed into 'The Laughing Sailor' or 'The Execution'. You could hang around those machines until someone else put the money in and then enjoy the show. In 'The Execution', the set was a house with many windows, quite unlike any prison, which opened in turn to show various scenes – the prisoner awaiting his fate, the parson reading from the Bible as the hooded victim stood on the scaffold with the rope around his neck, then the moment of the execution itself, when the poor fellow fell through a trap door and the grisly story came to an end. All the while, 'The Laughing Sailor' rocked around next door on his upturned barrel and roared with laughter. There must have been half a dozen other machines, but these two are the ones I remember.

On the sea front at Thorpe Bay, beyond Southend, was a row of trees, buffeted by the unrestrained sea gales. One was leaning at a dangerous angle. My brother John and I were convinced that it was bound to blow down. For a while, we rode our bicycles there each day to see what had happened to it. Unknown to me, John was using the tree as an excuse to get me out of the house while doctors visited my stricken father.

Then there were the boarding houses, like the one in Aberystwyth. Some had notices in their windows saying 'No Jews', or 'No Catholics'. Why? Why? No adult could give me an answer that made sense.

When I was six, the whole family set off for a day-trip to Herne Bay, the other side of the Thames. We went to the end of the pier, caught *The Golden Daffodil* and sat on coils of rope. A drunk man, with a flask of what I was assured was cold tea, danced around and told incomprehensible jokes, to our delight.

We trailed around Herne Bay, had a picnic lunch and ate ice creams. Then we saw that there was going to be a 'Talent Competition' at the bandstand! Great, I thought! I knew my parents wouldn't allow me to take part, so after we had all sat down in deck chairs, just as the Tommy Trinder look-a-like compere had asked for more competitors for the last time, I got up and ran like mad for the stage, with my mother in hot pursuit!

I clambered up and grabbed the man.

'I want to do something!' I told him.

'Mickey! Come down here at once!' shouted my mother from the front of the stalls.

'Go away!' I hissed back.

'Daddy says . . .' started my mother. But this was too much for the comedian.

'Don't worry, Mrs! We'll look after him. Won't we!' he added, turning to the crowd.

'Yes!' shouted back what seemed like a thousand voices. My mother retreated gracefully and I joined the gang of contestants.

'You stuck up little brat!' whispered a couple of teenage girls, who were flashing their teeth at the crowd to win them over.

Then I saw the prizes! There was a bicycle, a load of toys, and, to my delight, a beautiful rubber beach ball.

One by one, the contestants did their acts. The two girls sang 'Toot Toot Tootsie Goodbye' with a pre-rehearsed dance routine. An elderly lady, with a perpetual grin accompanied everyone on a stand up piano, as the sun beat down.

Then it was my turn.

'Hello, sonny. What's your name?'

He thrust a hand held microphone, like a metal toffee apple in my face.

'Mickey Wilcox.'

'Mickey! Mickey Mouse!' commented the razor witted comedian. 'What are you going to do for us, Mickey?'

'Sing a song.'

'What song?'

'About a donkey.'

'About a donkey?'

Laughter from the crowd. Sniggers from the bitchy girls.

'What's it called, Mickey?'

'I don't know.'

'You don't know?' He turned to Mabel at the piano and did his stage whisper, 'He doesn't know what it's called, Mabel!' Then he came back to me. 'And are you going to dance, Mickey?'

Dance? The idea appalled me. With half an eye on the beastly girls I grabbed the microphone and said, 'Only girls and sissies dance!'

Roars of laughter from the crowd, who, I feared, all wanted to play with my curly hair.

Then, without further delay, I sang my sad song about a donkey alone in a field at sunset, dreaming of better times. It was all of four lines long, but I thought it very moving and solemn. To me, the donkey was a real person, and I felt really sorry for him being left alone like that. As I sang, Mabel tried to follow the tune, which she couldn't possibly have heard before, on her piano. I finished and bowed deeply to the crowd, who responded with rapture, mingled with hysteria.

'Is that it, Mickey?' said the man.
'Yes. Can I do it again?'
'Can he?' shouted the comedian to the crowd.
'Yes!' they all shouted back.
'Can you ask the lady not to play the piano?' I asked politely.
More laughter.
'Did you hear that, Mabel?' said the man.
She nodded gracefully, still grinning half-wittedly.
'Why don't you want her to play, Mickey Mouse?' he asked.
'She doesn't know the tune.'
Who could deny it?

I sang my song again, even slower, milking every nuance of the tragic tale. Amidst further applause, I bowed even deeper than before.

When it came to the voting, to my delight, I won first prize. The girls were furious. To everyone's astonishment, I chose the beach ball.

'Don't you want the bicycle, Mickey?' said the bewildered comedian.

'No thank you, sir. I want the beach ball.'

'You idiot!' hissed the girls, who couldn't believe their luck.

So I caught *The Golden Daffodil* with my beach ball in my arms. The girls went off with the bicycle.

I played with my ball for some weeks on the beach at Westcliff. I used to throw or kick it into the sea and wait for the waves to bring it back to me. One day, the sea became tired of my game and took the ball far out of sight, back to Herne Bay, I shouldn't be surprised.

At Aberystwyth, the seminar (or was it a lecture?) turned into a verbal brawl. *Massage* is an uncomfortable, disturbing play. A middle-aged man admits that he has sexually abused a nine year old boy. He has hired the services of a heterosexual rent boy, who specialises in 'massage', who was himself severely and repeatedly abused by his step-father a few years earlier. The mixture is explosive.

What offended some of the students was the way the man tried to defend what he had done. They accused me of allowing him too much time to put his point of view. They wanted blood, retribution.

The debate soon went round in circles, with me saying that the play did not argue in favour of child abuse (of course!), while those against the play said it would encourage abusers (rubbish!), that it should have been about a male abuser of a small girl, not a boy ('You lifted the wrong corner of the carpet.' . . . interesting comment, I thought), that it was unfair to suggest that the boy's mother was in any way to blame for what had happened (I don't agree), and that I was wrong to give the man the last word in the matter (I don't, although it is true that he has the last extended speech).

Reading the text of a play, and seeing it in production are two different things. *Massage* is very complicated. What has actually happened? Are the characters giving us a true account of things? I doubt it. When you are reading a play, it is easy to forget that the person speaking is not the only character on the stage. How is Rikki, the rent boy, reacting to Dodge? Why do script readers continue to fall into the elementary trap of thinking what a character says is what the playwright believes?

I was asked why my characters didn't step forward from the action to make the political intention of the play less ambiguous? That's not my style. Not the way I write. I let my characters exist as themselves and not as mouthpieces for what I think. When Paul Blake addresses the audience in *Lent*, he does so as himself, for better or worse. Mary Mawson reads from her journal in *Accounts*, not mine or anyone else's. Creating a world within the drama, which has its own vitality and breathes its own air and is peopled by characters who have their own lives, is basic to a dramatist's craft. The world of *Massage* is one that has seldom (ever?) been dramatised in such detail. Its confusions and ambiguities are true to life in my experience.

Yet since writing the play, the Cleveland child abuse scandal has brought the sexual abuse of children into public consciousness and open debate. That *Massage* should pre-date Cleveland is coincidental. The passions expressed at the seminar were partly post-Cleveland hysteria and I was on the receiving end. I can cope with that. If I had written a murder mystery, violent death would not have aroused indignation to the same degree. Personally, I would prefer my own experience of sexual abuse to being murdered any day of the week. Our scale of values is out of balance because murder and violent death in drama are so common as to be unremarkable and seldom shocking, as they still are in real life, while sexual abuse is a hot and still taboo subject. *Massage* may be a less than perfect play, but if it shakes a few skeletons from the cupboard, it will have been worth its moment.

I am no stranger to censorial attitudes. I had a company of string puppeteers from the age of seven. My first plays were all for performance to the boarders at our school. We had a big hit with *The Witch's Christmas*!

The story concerned the Devil's attempts to dispatch an evil witch to Hell. But she was always too clever for him. So one Christmas, the Devil called at her home, pretending he was Father Christmas, and while the witch wasn't looking, he hid a sprig of holly behind one of her pictures. Off he went, leaving her a crate of beer. She had a marvellous time, playing dreadful tricks on everyone. She knew, however, that she had to clear away all Christmas decorations by Twelfth Night, or the Devil would get her! But she didn't know about the hidden sprig of holly. At the stroke of midnight, the Devil arrived, trailing fire and fury to claim her as his own!

The Witch's Christmas was a triumph! Oh! That I could conceive another plot with such unmistakable commercial mileage! The boys loved it. So did most of the staff. But the headmaster, who was in control of things after my father's death, treated our efforts with derision.

'The boys who like playing with dolls are doing something in the library after tea!' he announced with as listless a voice as he could muster.

But he hadn't bargained with our own advanced publicity machine! At a pre-arranged time, the school was plastered with posters, advertising the lurid play with pictures of a demented witch as far beyond the bounds of decency as our boyish imaginations could devise. Shrieks of laughter could be heard around the school. The headmaster's orders to tear down all the posters were carried out by reluctant teachers, who were roundly booed for their trouble.

For the master on duty, our performance was a gift. Every single boy was crammed into the library. All he had to do was sit back and enjoy the show.

There was more than just the play, of course. The rest of the bill was filled up with a dog, who pranced around the stage to the strains of 'How much is that doggy in the window?' (Roars of approval . . . act encored), followed by a Scotsman who drank and danced to Glen Miller's 'In the Mood'. At the end of the record, when the music seems to stop, then begins again, he would collapse as though comatosed, then, when the music suddenly started, he would leap up and dance even more furiously, before collapsing again. He was a SENSATION!

Then the play itself!

What a programme! What a hit!

Our fame spread, and we were invited to do our play at the local Primary School. We got the stage set up in their Hall, about a hundred and fifty children and teachers were assembled, then, and only then, did the headmistress demand to see the script. Fearing the worst, we denied that there was one. At least, it was in our heads, we told her. She stood her ground and demanded to know exactly what it was about. The audience was growing restless. I spluttered out the gist of the story, mentioning the witch (looking straight at her with narrowed eyes) and the Devil.

'Devil?' she roared.

Her pupils fell silent.

'Yes . . . you know . . . she's a very wicked witch and she goes to Hell. My play is very moral.'

'To Hell?' she spluttered. (This was the woman who dared to

stroke my hair and call me 'Curly'! My temper was rising!) 'You cannot bring the Devil into my school! You cannot speak of Hell in this place!' she growled.

For her pupils, what followed was at least as entertaining as the play itself. We had a furious row! She was evidently quite unused to having a small boy stand up to her, but as far as I was concerned, we had been invited to her school with our play and we were jolly well going to do it! She insisted that the Devil be called 'The Demon King' and Hell 'The Underworld'! We grudgingly agreed. Huge sighs of relief from her pupils.

Of course, we were as naughty as possible.

'Yes! I am indeed the Devil ... errr ... I mean The Demon King!'

'Oh do not take me to Hell!'

'Very well! You shall come to the Underworld instead!'

'Thank God for that!'

By this time we were all hysterical with laughter, our puppets swinging crazily in the air as we tried not to double up and fall off our platform behind the stage.

We were not asked back again.

But some of the boys waved and shouted at us around town for weeks afterwards. That was good!

My father was weak and bedridden for the last part of his life. He lay in his room at home, with a nurse and my mother at hand to give him oxygen when he needed it. I was shocked by his thin legs when he had a bed bath.

One parent, Mr Bulgin, very kindly gave him a prototype LP record player (this was 1950) and, as chance would have it, Decca's first batch of LPs included many of the Gilbert and Sullivan operas, which my father loved. Us children would sit outside his bedroom (in case we gave him an infection!) and follow *The Mikado*, *The Pirates of Penzance* and the rest in a book containing all the libretti of 'The Savoy Operas'. We loved the melodies, and the funny lines, and took the absurd plots rather seriously. At eight years old, I soon knew most of the scores by heart, words and music.

Just before the Christmas of 1950, my father suddenly decided to take us all to the Circus at the Southend Kursaal. We couldn't believe he was getting out of bed and dressing. 'Daddy must be getting better,' we whispered. My mother thought he was mad, but he insisted. 'If I can't take my children to the Circus at Christmas, what am I good for?' he argued.

He borrowed old Mrs Wilcox's car and off we set. Parking near the Kursaal proved impossible and we all had to walk miles, which weakened him.

'How are you feeling, Mickey?' he asked, suddenly.

We knew he was feeling dreadful. I wanted to make him laugh.

'I feel as fresh as a fish!' I said.

We were all very excited to be at the ringside. But after a short while, it was clear that my father was on the verge of collapse. My mother helped him from his seat, and we all tried to watch the clowns as though nothing had happened, but we were near to tears. While my father was given oxygen behind the scenes, we watched trapeze artists, and a lion tamer with a greasy body.

In the following February, Mr Bates, the choir master, told us that he had new folders to keep our music in. He picked me out.

'Wilcox, I think your father would be interested to see one. Take this, and see if he approves.'

I took the new folder up to his bedroom. There was considerable activity. The nurse was unwilling to let me in. After a whispered exchange, I was allowed into the bedroom. My father was propped up in bed and being given a warm drink from a glass in a plastic frame. His hands were shaking. He looked terrible.

'Mr Bates asked me to show you this.'

I showed him the music folder.

'Do you like it, Daddy? The boys think they're terrific! The choir's singing terribly well tonight!'

I was trying to be enthusiastic, but my heart was beating fast and I felt dizzy.

He turned his head towards the folder, with its Royal College of Music crest.

'Tell Bates . . . tell him . . . I'll speak to him . . . in the morning,' he murmured.

'Off you go, dear,' said the nurse.

I went back to the choir practice. Everyone fell silent as I entered.

'Daddy says they're very nice.'

'Oh! I am glad,' said Mr Bates.

We all knew what was happening.

My father died that night. We weren't told straight away. The nurse put a Victorian water jug by his bedroom door.

'I'm just putting that there, so you won't walk in and wake up your father,' she said feebly.

We played our part and went off to school. From my desk in 2B, I could look up at his bedroom window and I saw that the curtain remained drawn, confirming my worst fears.

At morning break, my mother called us to her bedroom, sat us in a row on the bed and told us that Father was dead. We each had a cup of coffee in the kitchen and went back to our classrooms. The other boys asked what had happened.

'Daddy's dead,' I whispered. They were very decent about it.

That evening, my young brother, Mark, ran round the empty school shouting 'I want my daddy back! You've hidden him! Where's my daddy?'

March

The BMA script about drug addiction has been received with enthusiasm! How splendid! What a change from the delays and tepid commitment of BBC TV. Somebody out there actually wants my work. Norman Burrows summoned me back to London to discuss another script in the same series. This time, a doctor has an HIV positive patient who has been fine for a number of years, but is starting to show signs that he may be in the first stages of AIDS.

At the meeting I was introduced to Hilary Curtis of the BMA, who outlined the specific medical conditions that the doctor might encounter, and who gave me a couple of books on the subject. One contained pages of gruesome colour photographs of many of the physical manifestations of AIDS.

Hilary, fierce, embattled, knows what she wants, but, like Norman, shows her inexperience at handling writers. We are not word processors on legs, waiting to be programmed, although we sometimes have to pretend that that is what we are. Since this work for the BMA is unpaid, financial incentives are not part of the package. I am motivated by the interest of the work itself, and what I am learning about the medical profession from the inside. But my devotion to duty is not inexhaustible.

What a relief to go to the *Opera Now* launch party. I was thrown into confusion about what I should wear. I belong to the generation that was brought up with post-war rationing. Most of my clothes were cast-offs from my older brother. There was never any question of spending my own small amount of pocket money on clothes. We wore the same things from one day to the next. Socks and underpants were changed once a week. Shirts once a fortnight. Trousers . . . once or twice a term? Coupled with one, or possibly two, baths a week, if we were lucky, we must have been very smelly children indeed.

The outcome of this has been that I am uneasy about buying clothes for myself, and resent having to do so. If I look like a walking advertisement for Marks and Spencer (one that they would not be keen to acknowledge, most probably) it's because their clothes are safe in style (plain dull?) and hard wearing. What I'm not bad at is choosing shoes and weather gear that makes sense in the country, so I clump around London in sturdy walking shoes and a 'Goretex' anorak.

But, oh dear, I couldn't go to the posh *Opera Now* launch in my cords! So off I went to M & S in Oxford Street to buy my way out of trouble. My new light-weight grey suit cost a staggering £120, for which I could have flown to New York! I chose the light-weight material because I thought it would be easier to travel with, and because the slinky trousers felt so wicked.

Back at 'The Filmworks' I pinched one of Tony's best shirts. He gets up at dawn to iron half a dozen of them, and brings tea in bed to the entire household, which is exactly how senior television executives ought to behave. Then it's a quick polish of my 'Mephisto' walking shoes, which I hoped nobody would see in the crush, and off to Soho.

The event itself was quite amusing. The string quartet in the gallery soon gave up, being drowned by disregard from below. The place was crammed with opera mafia, ranging from the regal to the divine. Make your own list of who was there.

I spoke to editor Mel Cooper's elderly father.

'I can't make head or tail of my son. I've come to the conclusion he's no good! God knows what he's up to this time!'

I buzzed around chatting to people I didn't know, who looked as lost as I felt. Then, after about two hours, the whole crowd melted away, and that was that. I suppose most of the others there go to so many events that they regard them as a duty rather than a pleasure. But not me! I seldom get invited to anything, and could have done with a bit more fun. I tried my best.

Too soon, I was tucked into my warm, bright red (so I can be more easily seen by rescue helicopters) 'Goretex' anorak, and was marching, new suit and all, through dark and rainy Soho. Boo!

I like to catch the 9 am train from King's Cross back to Newcastle. If all goes well, I can be back in my house by 2.30 pm. But all didn't go well. When I got to the place where my car should have been parked, all I found was a small pile of glass. For the second time in six months, my car had been stolen.

There was all the hassle of contacting the police and getting things sorted out. Last time, my car was a total write-off. This time, the police had been called and the damage to my new car was not terminal. Nevertheless, it was locked away in a garage for the weekend in its vandalised state. There was nothing for it but to catch another train out to Haltwhistle and then walk the four miles out to my cottage, up the South Tyne valley.

Thank Heavens for my rucksack and wet weather gear. It may look odd in London, but it makes sense in the real world.

I was up early on Monday and got to work on the new BMA script. By 3.30 pm the first draft was finished. Rather than send it off that day, I thought I'd sleep on it and do some revisions the following morning before walking into Haltwhistle to send it off.

At 10.30 that night I got a phonecall from Norman Burrows asking me if I would catch the first train down to London the next day!

'Sorry to lean on you, Michael. We're in a spot of bother with another script in the BMA series. The writer has gone on holiday and we start filming in ten days. Our director wants some re-writes. You could bring the HIV script with you and save the postage!'

'Who is your director?'

'Someone called Nick Hamm.'

'Nick Hamm? The theatre director? Used to be with the Royal Shakespeare Company?'

'Did he?'

'Yes, Norman! He runs the Lilian Baylis at the moment.'

Norman, evidently, hadn't a clue who his director was. Neither did he understand my problem of getting anywhere with my car wrecked. And what started off as a one off fifteen-minute play (for no fee, since the BMA's Foundation for AIDS is a charity) was ending up as three dramas (for nothing times three!).

Why am I doing this?

This time it was simply a question of back-packing my way to Haltwhistle and letting British Rail get me there on time. During the journey, I was reading David Cairns's new biography of Hector Berlioz for an *Opera Now* article.

Once at the London offices of Software Production Enterprises, we all read through the offending script with Nick Hamm. It was obvious that a complete re-write was the only answer. I got a short briefing, and some information was faxed through from Hilary Curtis at the BMA, then I was out in the street again . . .

. . . and back to Newcastle, reading more of *Berlioz* on the way. Then a two-mile walk to Byker to pick up my repaired car, and then the hour-long drive out to my house in the hills.

First thing the next day, I got up early to write the third play for the BMA in a single sitting! This time, there was even less time to be lost, and as soon as I'd done it, I drove into Haltwhistle and faxed it through to the SPE offices. So in the space of four days I'd written and delivered two complete scripts and made a round trip to London.

Then the trouble began.

One of the characters in Anon's rejected script was a homosexual man who, in that version, was attempting to get Life Insurance. He was portrayed as a miserable wretch, who was last seen entering a hospital's casualty unit with AIDS! I thought this was deplorable and homophobic and said so. In my version, he was portrayed as being healthy, successful and monogamous, with his barrister lover.

Hilary Curtis was on the phone in a flash.

'You can't show a homosexual couple that is so successful!' she said.

'Why?'

'The doctors will bitterly resent it! They are mostly homophobic. They will be infuriated to see a pair of homosexuals living better than they do!'

'But Hilary, doctors are amongst the better paid people . . .'

'No they aren't!'

'How much do they get paid then?'

'There are plenty of doctors getting less than £30,000 a year!'

'Isn't that quite good pay?'

'They don't think so!'

'There are plenty of doctors getting more than £30,000, aren't there?'

'Never mind. You can't show a pair of happy, successful homosexuals!'

And so on.

I had also made one or two technical errors about blood donors and kidney donor cards that I was happy to correct.

Is this the best the latter part of the twentieth century has to offer? Hilary Curtis was apologetic, as well she should be, but the fact remains that this particular homosexual is furious and insulted. Why shouldn't a homosexual be a happy, responsible and successful human being? Why should doctors, of all people, find the notion of a homosexual, healthy in mind and body, so objectionable? The BMA is happy to make use of this homosexual's skills and have him travelling back and forth while he could be spending his time earning his own living, but apparently he's supposed to fuel the homophobia of the BMA and its members. Thanks a lot!

No way was I going to return to the bedraggled gay of the previous version. So a wretched compromise was agreed. Our homosexual could be healthy and successful, but could not be shown with his lover or in a too luxurious home! A most unsatisfactory sort of victory.

Meanwhile, I managed to see the second of only two performances of *Brats* by the Haltwhistle Young Farmers. They had come seventh out of seven at the competition in Hexham a few days previously. This time they were performing for local charities at Haltwhistle Middle School.

The audience consisted mostly of friends and family of the performers, which meant that the hall was quite full. I had not seen anything of the work on the play since the read-through. I was disappointed by what I saw and could easily understand why they had not done better at Hexham. *Brats* was torture to sit through and looked like unbelievably bad work. Nevertheless, Haltwhistle YFC had made the effort to do something, unlike many other clubs in the region. But that didn't stop me feeling as though I had been mugged. I had a cricket club committee meeting the same evening, and slipped away, grim faced, during the coffee and raffle break.

I once saw a plane explode in the sky a few hundred feet above my head.

I had just had my ninth birthday and was playing on the school field with my friend, David. Every year, there was a Battle of Britain fly-past over the wartime airbase of Biggin Hill. The planes used to assemble in the air and fly over Southend on their way south to Kent. There were Spitfire fighters and Lancaster bombers and heaven knows what else, and they made most sinister music.

When David and I heard an aircraft approaching, of course we looked up to identify it. But this time, the sound it made was alarming. It seemed very close, but we couldn't see it. There was a moment of real fear before the plane suddenly appeared from behind roof tops. It was very low and smoke was pouring from a sick engine.

We could see the pilot. He was turning in the cockpit, as though trying to find a way out. Then the plane blew apart. We saw bits of it whizzing in all directions. There was no noise at first. Then there was a tremendous bang! The wreckage crashed into houses behind the Mascot Cinema on the London Road. We ran towards the crash site, which was a few hundred yards away, and got there before the police and ambulances arrived.

All the windows in the street were broken by the explosion, and a row of four or five terraced houses were demolished by crashing wreckage.

Lots of other people were running to the spot. An old lady came out of one of the houses.

'Has the war started again, lovey?'

'A plane crashed! It blew up! We saw it!' I told her.

She looked at her broken windows.

'Look at them! I just cleaned the buggers this morning! Mustn't grumble. I'll put the kettle on!'

Further down the street, the main body of the fuselage was still in one piece, its nose stuck in the road. There were bits of plane all over the place. Police and ambulances arrived and we watched as chains of people started to tear away at the debris of the demolished houses. One man was brought out on a stretcher and passed down from hand to hand. It was a scene from the blitz, of recent memory to those involved, recreated before my eyes.

There were ambulance men and nurses all over the place with nothing to do. We learnt later that, miraculously, no one on the ground had been killed and the houses flattened by the aircraft were empty, apart from the unfortunate man on the stretcher. Feeling that the ambulances were missing out on the excitement, I thought it was my duty to offer myself as a disaster victim. So I hobbled up and said my foot hurt (quite untrue) and a swarm of uniforms buzzed around me, taking off my shoe and sock and inspecting my dirty foot, on which there wasn't a mark. After playing my part so convincingly, the least they could have done was give me a bandage, but it was not to be.

'Go home, curly-top! This is no place for you!'

I went red with humiliation. But I saw the whole thing! I was first on the scene! I'd even gone out of my way to give them a casualty to treat! And all he could do was call me 'Curly-top' in front of all those people!

I ran off towards a crowd that had gathered round the main body of the fuselage and met a teacher I knew.

'Don't go near the crowd. Someone might light a cigarette. They might panic and you'd get crushed or trampled.'

'Are there any dead bodies?'

'There must be somewhere.'

'I saw him,' I said.

'Who?'

'The pilot. He turned round in the cabin. Before it blew up.'

'You saw it blow up?'

'Yes. Was he . . . ?' I was about to ask a stupid question. 'He was killed,' I said.

My BMA script was recorded on video last week. Poor Richard O'Callaghan, who was to have played a whizz-kid businessman, was told his hair was too long for the part. (It wasn't THAT long!) Hilary Curtis, the 'client' in this production, thought that her doctors would be offended to see someone with longish hair working in a city investment company, so Richard was replaced. Both Nick Hamm and I would have used him like a shot, straggly hair and all. He's a wonderful actor.

Nick's thoroughness seemed to surprise the production staff (not the actors, most of whom had worked with him before). By the end of the day he was running forty-five minutes over time. Not bad from an artistic point of view, but a problem for the producer. We were working in the Citicorp Building, on the south east bank of the Thames. Our presence there was not insured after 6 pm. Would the camera crew ask for extra expenses for running over time? Would the tiny budget run out before day three?

On day two, we were in the same building. Mid-afternoon, producer Norman Burrows looked at me with drawn face and said: 'Do we have a film?'

'You're asking the wrong person,' I whispered.

By the third and final day, the Company Manager was peevish and referred to Nick as 'Zeffirelli'. Hilary Curtis of the BMA entered into the spirit of things excellently and was a positive help in tightening up parts of my script. When I left for Northumberland at lunch time, everything seemed to be going well. We did indeed have a film.

Or so I thought . . .

I got back to my cottage at 8.30 that night. I'd left my car at home, not wishing to find another pile of broken glass in Newcastle. So I had to back-pack my way from Haltwhistle Station after the five-hour journey once again. I was dizzy with tiredness, but I knew I had to put in an appearance at the

Haltwhistle Cricket Club annual do at the Comrades' Club. So it was a quick shower, a change of clothes and out again. I managed to last an hour and a half at the Club. A comedy duo from Carlisle included racist, sexist and homophobic jokes in their act.

Ugly laughter.

I left the Comrades' Club and went, exhausted, to bed.

After my father's death, when I was nine years old, Mr Noble, who had been joint headmaster, took over the day-to-day running of the school. My older brother, John, went away to Malvern College in Worcestershire. My sister, Sally, was at one of her many, dreadful boarding schools, and my young brother, Mark, was still a toddler.

I was on my own, not quite living as a boarder, since the school was my home and I had my own bedroom, but not as a dayboy either. I don't blame some of the genuine boarders for resenting my privileged status, as it must have seemed to them. But it was not a situation of my own making. Given the choice, I would rather have been captured by pirates and bid farewell to the whole damn thing.

But that happy circumstance (which might have included a few problems of its own) was not to be. With my father and my family out of the way, I was prey to the vicious whims of Mr Noble. To those who know *Lent*, this scenario may be familiar.

Mr Noble's regard for our puppet company, and his enlightening leavers' talk might appear eccentrically dotty, rather than malign. However, I was on the receiving end of a series of nasty, boyish cruelties for which he was primarily responsible.

On one occasion, I was summoned, out of the blue, to the front of the whole school at morning assembly and accused by him of stealing. I denied any such thing. He then got a boy I'll call Tomkins to step forward to corroborate his accusations. This really astonished me, because Tomkins knew he was lying and so did 99 per cent of the other boys. Nevertheless, Mr Noble persisted in his charges, whilst I continued to deny them, accusing Tomkins, with Biblical theatricality, of 'bearing false witness' for which he was sure to burn in Hell! I was trembling with rage and frustration. Some of the teachers present were so shocked by what was happening, that they marched noisily from the hall in protest. Mr Noble saw that he was losing the initiative and sent Tomkins and myself back to our places. He never mentioned the matter again.

As we filed out of assembly, two of the younger teachers took me on one side.

'We know what's going on. We know you didn't do it,' they told me.

When I got to my classroom, I asked Tomkins, in front of the other boys, why he had lied. He shook his head and started to weep quietly. What hold Mr Noble had over him, I dread to guess.

Some weeks later, Tomkins was missing at lunch. The word went round the room in a flash! Tomkins had run away! The odd thing was that I liked Tomkins and felt really sorry for him. I put up my hand and asked the master on duty if I could go and look round the school to find him.

Along with a few other boys, I searched everywhere. Eventually, I found him hiding behind the gymnasium. He was terribly unhappy and crying. I told him everything would be all right and that lunch wasn't that bad!

'What is it?' he sobbed.

I put my arm around him.

'It's corned beef, mashed potatoes and beetroot. Only you'd better hurry, because they'll soon be doing second helpings and they'll eat yours!'

'I don't want any!'

'Well I do, and I'm not going to eat mine until you come back!'

'Who's on duty?'

'Mr Harrison. He's OK.'

'What else is there?'

'Frogspawn, with a blob of jam!'

'I don't like frogspawn.'

'Well I love it! It's so deliciously slimy!'

He started to laugh through his sobs, making him heave and gasp. We walked back to the dining hall with our arms round each other's shoulders. He went to his place and was given his plate of corned beef. The boys were quiet for a moment, then started chattering again.

I had to go to my own place, on a table apart.

In the week following the BMA shoot, Nick Hamm was busy editing the film. I soon started getting furious phonecalls, mostly after midnight, from Nick. He told me that he was being harassed by Dr John Dawson of the BMA's Foundation for AIDS. Scenes which had been approved at the script stage were now under attack, particularly one in which Arnold, my homosexual photographer, was seen with a Life Insurance agent and being discriminated against because he admitted to being gay.

The result was that Nick was required to cut most of the scene. By the time I saw it, there was no way of telling who the Insurance man was (he might have been a doctor, or anything for that matter) and the point of the scene was lost. The same sort of arguments that had been used against the two gay lovers on my first draft, and Richard O'Callaghan's longish hair, were used again. Doctors seeing the film might be offended and lose sympathy with the film. In short, it seemed that blatant homophobia was being appeased yet again.

To say Nick Hamm was furious is to do him an injustice. He was raving, ranting mad! I have never heard such shouting and yelling on my phone before. He thought he had the makings of a fascinating and original drama which was being dismembered before his eyes.

When it became clear that Nick's jazzy and fun opening sequence was going to suffer the same fate, and that the computer virus theme that I had introduced also had the surgeon's knife poised above it, to say nothing of the closing shot of Arnold Lawrence taking a photograph of the doctors, I thought poor Nick would self-combust!

In my original draft, Stefan, the barrister, was telling his lover about his day in Norwich:

> STEFAN ... then the Judge asked why my client thought the public deserved to see 'DEKKA' – that was the accused's street name – in rainbow colours, five feet tall. The boy said, 'Trees are too precious to carve my name on!' I'd have acquitted him on the spot!
>
> (Cut from *On the Record*: BMA video)

When Stefan was removed from my script, I gave the speech to Lawrence, the homosexual photographer. It gave the piece a curious, off-beat ending, with a boy at street level trying to leave a record of his existence. Sadly, that too ended up on the editing room floor.

'Michael! You've got to do something about this!' screamed Nick.

'I shall ... in my own way,' I said quietly.

I reckoned that it was better to fight my corner from within, than walk out in a rage.

While all this was boiling away in Soho, I was in Northumberland, busily writing about David Cairns's splendid Berlioz biography, meeting a tight deadline over Simon Rattle's new recording of Gershwin's *Porgy and Bess* (both for *Opera Now* magazine) and preparing a performing script of C. P. Taylor's complicated play *Bandits* for a forthcoming production by Newcastle's Live Theatre Company.

After preparing his own, compromised cut of the BMA film, Nick was told by the Trustees of the Foundation for AIDS that *On the Record* was not acceptable in its present form. There then followed an extraordinary scene in which Dr John Dawson and Norman Burrows re-edited Nick's cut, while Nick sat in the editing room at the back, telling them both what a couple of shits they were!

Nick was on the phone to me, once again, at half past midnight.

'How can you sit up there and let them do this to your script,

Michael?' he screamed. 'It's a fucking farce! It's fucking appeasement of fucking homophobic doctors! They're cowards, both of them! Fucking timid, gutless, wanking, small minded FUCKERS! They've ruined my film. I've demanded to have my name removed from the credits. You should do the same. For Christ's sake, Michael, what are you going to do?'

'They're sending me your cut in the morning. I want to see it first.'

It arrived mid-morning. I thought a lot of it was OK. Some bits didn't make sense (the Insurance man scene, now cut to ribbons) and the computer virus scene didn't come off (partly my fault . . . not enough dialogue). Anyway, by this time, the film had been recut and dispatched to the Wellcome Foundation, I learned later. As it stood in Nick's cut, the film was unsatisfactory in part, although the surgery scenes and much of the work elsewhere were good.

I had not seen the Burrows/Dawson cut and reserved judgment, although if the scene between Arnold Lawrence and his doctor had been cut, then it would have been my turn to hit the roof!

DR RICE *is seeing* ARNOLD LAWRENCE *in her surgery*.

LAWRENCE I've seen five lots of Life Insurance people. I've now found one company that's prepared to offer terms, subject to your medical report.

RICE Right.

LAWRENCE What I need to know is whether my medical report is going to . . . you know . . .

RICE Obviously I cannot speak for the Insurance Company, Arnold. I can only speak as your doctor.

LAWRENCE Stefan and I . . . we're not high risk. We've been together now for ten years.

RICE How is Stefan?

LAWRENCE Busy. He's got a case in Norwich today.

RICE So you're both doing well?

LAWRENCE Yes.

RICE Excellent.

LAWRENCE When this whole AIDS business became big news over here, homosexuals were asked to stop giving blood and not to carry kidney donor cards. I'd carried a card since I was sixteen. I threw it in the fire. I was upset. Insulted. My kidneys are healthy. But I'm told just because I'm homosexual I'm a danger. I knew that was rubbish. But I still had to burn my card.

RICE This Medical Report . . . doctors must not speculate, any more than witnesses in a Court of Law are permitted to express opinion. When I compile a Medical Report, it contains fact only, not guesswork, prejudicial comment, or speculation. Only certifiable, scientifically determined facts about the patient.

LAWRENCE So the fact that I am homosexual does not automatically brand me as a high risk person?

RICE A homosexual might be in a high risk category, but so might a heterosexual. It would all depend on the facts, not prejudice or speculation.

LAWRENCE Would you have to say that a patient was homosexual?

RICE If I knew that for a fact, and it was relevant to the questions I was being asked, I would mention that a patient was homosexual.

LAWRENCE And therefore 'high risk'?

RICE No. Not necessarily. In your case, and I've known you and Stefan for some years, I would not automatically describe you as 'high risk'.

(From *On the Record*: BMA video)

Remember that this video will be shown to doctors, and that its purpose is to provide information on the new Act concerning a patient's rights of access to Medical Reports. I reckoned that it was more important to stick with the project and see a scene like this included in the final version, as indeed it was (played excellently by Jay Villiers and Celia Imrie) than walk out in a rage and risk having it cut.

But where this wretched episode leaves my other two BMA scripts remains to be seen.

The cricket season starts in three weeks' time. During the winter months, money has been raised by various means, including Ali Milburn's 'Sports Quiz' and a lucky numbers Draw (10 pence a card). Work gangs have been down at the ground, scarrifying, then rolling, the square. New equipment has been bought at Penrith during a Friday night team outing, like a cricketers' Tupperware Party.

But the Young Farmers have created an outrage by holding a Jumble Sale in the town two weeks before the traditional date of the Cricket Club Jumble Sale! Ours has had to be postponed till mid-June, but there will be some fierce exchanges at the next Committee meeting!

Meanwhile, as Second team captain this season, I have had a team and tactics meeting with vice-captain, Tom Lee, and last year's captain, Eddie Howe.

We made a list of all the players in the club and figured out what our XI might look like and who would be opening the bowling and batting. I wanted young Chris Smith to take over as wicket keeper. Chris is seventeen and very promising. I wanted, as a matter of policy, to encourage the young players as much as possible. To this end, I also said that I wanted Graham Lee, Tom's sixteen-year-old son and our Junior captain, to open the batting. Other promising young players include Neil Robinson and Andrew Taylor, both still juniors in age, but young adults in my eyes.

In the West Tyne League, we play forty-two over matches in a season that starts in the third week in April and ends in the middle of September. I discussed with Tom and Eddie my conviction that we should set targets for the opening batsmen to reach (thirty runs off the first ten overs) and have a flexible batting order, whereby we never had two slow scoring batsmen in together. Instead, I wanted to get my 'hitmen' to the crease in plenty of time to do their quick scoring.

Too often, limited over games are dominated by batsmen who have sound defences but slow scoring rates. This leaves the rest of the team having to bat the last few overs and thrash about before they've got their eyes in, with often dispiriting results.

Heavens! What does it take to drive home the obvious fact that runs win limited over matches?

April

My resentment of Mr Noble, the headmaster of our school, increased as his mean and petty acts continued. As a result, I became more isolated, spending many days fishing on my own in a small lake near Hadleigh, and reading books about prisoners of war. I found it easy to identify with the prisoners, who seemed to speak and act like schoolboys most of the time. And it was obvious that Mr Noble was the 'goon' in charge.

I also collected Classic Comics, in which great novels of world literature were re-told in imaginative cartoons. In this form, I was introduced to *Uncle Tom's Cabin*, *The Talisman*, *The Fall of the House of Usher*, *Crime and Punishment* and many other novels that I would never have read in their original form.

Collecting became, and has remained, an obsession. My library of war books was carefully catalogued and arranged on a special shelf, my fishing tackle and past issues of *Angling Times* were constantly inspected and stored, and my Classic Comic collection was loaned out to interested boarders, their names and the date of the loan being entered in an old exercise book, like an efficient library service.

Today, my extensive LP collection is carefully shelved, details of my CD collection are stored in a computer database, and all the letters, contracts and various drafts of my scripts are stacked away in folders. Back issues of magazines sit in chronological heaps for easy reference. I have read every issue of *Gramophone* magazine from cover to cover since 1956, when I was thirteen years old.

In the 1950s, Alleyn Court had an extensive collection of 78 rpm records, as well as a better than average electrical system to play them on (also a gift from the same, generous Mr Arthur Bulgin, who gave my father the early LP player). During term time, Music Club was after tea every Sunday, and the master on duty would present an hour of music (entirely 'classical') from the collection.

'The Arrival of the Queen of Sheba' was explained to us as though it were programme music (which it isn't!). We were puzzled and said that we couldn't see her getting out of the boat. Surely we should be able to hear the sea, then the crowd applauding her as she disembarked, and then some music suitable for someone who had just come from Sheba?

'Please sir? Where exactly is "Sheba"?'

He obviously had no idea.

'Look it up in the Bible! Now we'll have Haydn's Trumpet Concerto . . . third movement . . . played by Sir Harry Mortimer!'

'Has he been knighted, sir?'

'Oh yes, sir! Is he now SIR Harry, sir?'

The teacher squinted at the record label.

'Hold on! Oh, with all due respect, according to the label, he still awaits that honour. Overdue, I should say.'

'Yes, sir! He's a jolly good trumpeter, isn't he, sir!'

'Sir? Can we have the second movement? We had the third last Sunday.'

'Oh shut up! The second's hopeless! Play the third, sir!'

'Why can't we have "Tiger Rag", sir?'

'Because it's Sunday!'

'But what's wrong with Jazz on a Sunday, sir?'

'It's not Christian music.'

'But the Queen of Sheba wasn't a Christian, sir.'

'And she'd been travelling on a Sunday, sir!'

'Sunday is the day of rest, sir!'

The teacher was beginning to look frayed.

'I wish it was!' he mumbled. 'Anyway, the Queen of Sheba couldn't have been a Christian. She's in the Old Testament,' he added with a twinkle.

'Mr Jones said she was a harlot surrounded by catamites, sir,' added Snooks, helpfully.

'What's a catamite, sir?'

Halsey major was a real know-all.

'They're boys who lie on cushions all day eating grapes,' he told us.

'Golly, sir!' shrieked Wakeling, 'Can we be catamites when we grow up?'

'Right! Silence! Haydn's Trumpet Concerto!'

And so on.

Thus Gigli, Joan Hammond, Peter Dawson, Mozart and Elgar all meant something to us at an early age. And in the holiday time, I had uninterrupted access to all the records, like Paul Blake in *Lent*.

> PAUL I've discovered some more music, Matey!
> MATEY Oh?
> PAUL There are only two records left out of the original set. It's Elgar's Violin Concerto. Elgar's actually conducting! There's the slow movement and the end of the last movement. There used to be six records, Matey. The rest are lost or bust. The music is very strange, and I don't really understand it. But I have to keep going back to it. It's really weird!
> MATEY And do you know the name of the violinist?
> PAUL Menuhin.
> MATEY He was just a little older than you when he made that recording.
> PAUL Is he still alive?
> MATEY Very alive.
> PAUL And Elgar?
> MATEY Very dead.
> PAUL I'm going to search through the record shops and find the missing records!
> MATEY If you find any of them, buy them, whatever the price, and I will pay you back. Will you let me do that?
> PAUL Thank you, sir.

(From *Lent*)

I travelled down to London for a few days to see the first of my BMA videos, now titled *On the Record* by someone. Prior to the showing, to which the cast and crew and various dignitaries had been invited, there was a lengthy meeting between John Dawson and Hilary Curtis of the BMA, Norman Burrows of Software Production Enterprises and myself. I had already had quite a bit to say to Norman the day before about what had been going on during the filming. I emphasised the importance of working on the script thoroughly before shooting, so that time and money wasn't wasted. There is no point in approving a script, then cutting it to bits during post-production, as had happened with *On the Record*.

On the subject of homophobia, I suggested that John Dawson should give an interview to *Gay Times* so that the aims and policies of the Foundation for AIDS could be clearly expressed. He agreed and the next day I contacted the features editor of *Gay Times*, Peter Burton, to arrange this.

We then read through both my other BMA scripts and I noted a few sensible challenges, promising to prepare new drafts of each for the following week. I now expect the scripts to be recorded in full and without editorial tampering.

The launch reception was also (and far more importantly) for the late Paul Sieghart's last book, *AIDS and Human Rights*, which was also commissioned by the BMA's Foundation for AIDS. It was a particular pleasure to meet the author's widow and son, and to say how much I valued the book, which I had read that morning.

A number of the actors from *On the Record* were there, and after the showing, Hilary Curtis was challenged by Celia Imrie, Jay Villiers and Ninka Scott, who all thought that appeasing homophobes was a bad policy.

'You don't appease such people,' insisted Jay Villiers, 'You challenge them! Confront them!'

Hilary explained her point of view, and the problems of trying to win over arch conservatives. The truth is that you can't change some people, however hard you try. And by appeasing evil, which is what homophobia is, you are condoning it. What a tragedy that Paul Sieghart wasn't present to add to this important debate.

I was assured by Norman Burrows that Nick Hamm had been sent an invitation, and I was sorry not to see him there. The policy of standing your ground and arguing your case, adopted by Celia, Jay, Ninka and myself, is surely the best one in such circumstances. No one who has read *AIDS and Human Rights* need ever doubt the good intentions of the BMA's Foundation for AIDS.

My early acts of anarchy were not carefully planned. I was playing with another boy, who I'll call Fulton. We had been collecting fireworks for 5 November and were busily laying them out in order and studying the packaging and instructions of each. The anticipation of what they might do, when the blue touch paper was lit, added to the excitement of the build up to Bonfire Night. So with 'Vesuvius' we imagined seeing a small volcano erupt before our eyes, and debated how many 'Star Bombs' might be thrown high into the air from each firework. Penny bangers and jumping jacks were the best value. Rockets cost between 3d and 1/6d as far as we were concerned, although 'The Argosy' had some costing far more. Considering our pocket money was still fixed at 1/- a week, quantity rather than quality made most sense.

As we examined our collection, the boarders were doing 'prep' (homework) in the classroom beneath us. In a fit of devilment, Fulton and I decided to drop lighted bangers down the drainpipes next to the 'prep' classrooms, to liven things up. We each held a banger and dared each other to be the first, holding out a lighted match for the other to set the short fuses fizzing.

Once lit, there was no turning back! Our explosives were dropped down the drainpipes, and then went off with thunderous effect! The master on duty rushed to the window to see who was there, but, of course, he couldn't know that the fireworks had been dropped from above. So Fulton and I escaped undetected.

We had thought that the boarders would enjoy this little escapade. But, in fact, many were frightened, especially one boy who was sitting near the window, who was quite hysterical. So our little prank soon achieved the status of an outrage!

I was out of love with authority, not surprisingly, and so, for different reasons, was Fulton. But I don't think either of us were prepared for the witch hunt that followed. At Prayers the next morning, Mr Noble threatened dreadful reprisals if the culprits didn't own up. 'Owning up' was always considered the right and honourable thing to do, but neither Fulton nor I was feeling honourably disposed. After all, I had read Conrad's *The Secret Agent* in the Classic Comics series, and argued that there was no point in being an anarchist if you were going to run to the nearest police station after your bomb had gone off!

So Fulton and I brazened it out, lying through our teeth to everyone, even though we were the prime suspects. One boy claimed that he had seen us doing the deed, even though we were well out of sight. Never since have I trusted the evidence of eye witnesses.

Interestingly, none of Mr Noble's threats came to pass. Our teachers liked half-holidays and Friday Film Nights as much as the boys and didn't see why they should be punished along with the rest of the school.

Although we got away with it, both Fulton and I were unhappy about what we had done. We never trusted each other again and our friendship evaporated and it has taken nearly forty years for me to confess that I was indeed The Mystery Bomber.

One week before the start of the cricket season!

The skies have cleared. The field is drying out. Alan Robson, who cares for the ground, has been hard at work. Each evening, from Sunday through till Friday, there have been nets and fielding practice. The age of players ranges from thirteen to somewhere in the region of fifty. The best of the Haltwhistle Juniors, such as Graham Lee, the Junior captain, and Andrew Taylor, his vice-captain, are keen to get selection for the Second team. Graham is certainly in, as a medium paced, left arm bowler and opening batsman. Andrew, an excellent all-round sportsman, gets selected for Saturday's match as a good fielder and sturdy striker of the ball.

At the end of each practice session, I drive Andrew Taylor back to his house, and anyone else who needs a lift.

'I'd really like to be a games teacher,' says Andrew, who is still a pupil at Haydon Bridge High School. Andrew is sixteen, but seems older. For some reason, which I've never understood, he has the nick-name of Mouse. Anyone less like a mouse is hard to imagine.

'See you on Saturday, Mike,' he says, as he carries his gear into the house.

At 9.30 am, on the day of the first match, the telephone rings. It is John Clark from Featherstone Castle.

'I have some sad news for you. Andrew Taylor . . . you know . . . Mouse . . . has been killed.'

'What happened?'

'Apparently, he was walking back, late last night, along the A69 from The Castle Club and was knocked down by a taxi. That's all I know.'

The whole community was in a state of shock when I went into town. Our match was rained off and the following week's Junior fixture postponed. Many tears were shed. Andrew's funeral was packed and his grave is still covered with flowers.

Everyone loved him.

The fields around my house are farmed by Tom Teasdale and his father, Coulson Teasdale. I have known Tom since he was a lad, just starting at Haydon Bridge Secondary School. Now he is married with three children, who are growing up fast. Tom was busy with the Young Farmers Club when I bought High Maidenway ten years ago. He was in the thick of football, tug of war, Cumberland wrestling, stock judging, drama, and everything else you can think of. He played an old mole catcher in *The Tups of High Cross Farm*, which became the closing scene of Act One of *Accounts*.

The mole catcher was written out of the full length play, but reappears in Act Two of *Tornrak*, the opera libretto that I have written for John Metcalf and the Welsh National Opera Company. After escaping from a travelling fair, Milak, an Inuit girl, lives wild in the Welsh mountains. The mole catcher she encounters admires her trapping skills, and the snares that she has made from rabbits' guts. They recognise in each other a distant kinship before Milak is forced to flee for her life.

A 'tup' is a ram, or male sheep, a 'yow' being a ewe. At the end of *Accounts*, one of the brothers confesses to the other that he is 'more interested in tups than yows', expressing his sexual interest in men rather than women. In spite of the fact that the word 'tup' is glossed endlessly in the script (even more so in the Film on Four production), this line has caused great confusion. After the première performance of *Accounts* at the Hudson Guild Theatre in New York, I overheard an elderly couple discussing the play.

'But what was Donald telling his brother at the end?' asked the mystified lady.

'He was saying he preferred sheep to women, my dear!'

This year, the winter has been as mild as I can remember, with scarcely any snow and few frosts even. Lambing is in full swing. Lambs are delightful, full of curiosity and play. Why, you may wonder, do they grow up (those that are allowed to) such dull creatures? The answer is all to do with food supply and survival. The lambs are fed a rich milk diet by their mothers, which means that they have time to gambol round the fields, discovering what the world is made of and having fun. If they get hungry or thirsty, all they have to do is run to mother. But when they grow up, they have to eat, eat and eat grass to survive. Life becomes one long chew. There is no time for play. Survival becomes the dullest of routines. Their sense of adventure and inventiveness is stifled. Lambs become sheep.

The same thing can happen to humans.

I have just been told that *Tornrak* will not now be produced by the Welsh National Opera in October, but in the summer of 1990 instead. I am very disappointed about this, but it is suggested that the opera will receive more performances and play in more venues next year than it would have done in this.

I have heard nothing from the composer, John Metcalf, since last year and I am wondering why?

This unusual commission came about because of the interest of Brian McMaster, the WNO Managing Director, in my stage plays. Brian was also aware of my interest in opera from *78 Revolutions* (a good idea, poorly developed by me, about the early days of the gramophone). We met in the sunken, marble tea room of the Adelphi hotel in the Strand where he introduced me to John Metcalf. John and I were then left alone and drank tea for two hours, trying to get to know one another.

I suggested various ideas for our proposed opera, including the history of the Atomic Bomb (about which I had written one of my first plays) and the death of Antinous, Hadrian's lover, who died in mysterious circumstances in the Nile. The first suggestion aroused some curiosity, the second none at all. We ended up deciding nothing for certain, except that we would continue to try and think of an idea.

Eventually, I started work on a libretto about two young Welsh brothers, who came to London to seek work and ended up as heroin addicts, sleeping rough.

Meanwhile, John was in the process of leaving the Arts Centre, where he worked in Wales, and moving with his family to the Banff Centre in Alberta, Canada, with its internationally renowned music theatre department. He had also seen a Theatre in Education (T.I.E.) programme in Wales about a cabin boy, shipwrecked in the Arctic, who was rescued by an Inuit girl, Milak. After various adventures, the cabin boy was rescued and brought back to Britain with the young girl. This was based on the true story of Mikak, who was brought to Britain by British sailors to become the subject of ethnic and anthropological study.

John thought this would make an excellent basis for an opera, and I agreed.

I wrote a rough draft of Act One, which included such exotic notions as a chorus of Husky dogs, a singing seagull and a polar bear hunt. This raised a few eyebrows in Cardiff, who had commissioned this new opera as a fringe production, playing around a few Arts centres and small venues in Wales.

I then flew out to Banff, up in the Rocky Mountains, read through a pile of books that John had gathered about Inuit culture, re-wrote Act One, and completed a draft of Act Two. A major addition to the narrative was the introduction of 'tornraks', or the spirits of animals. I also added the spirits of dead hunters and the busybody grandmother of Milak. 'Oh good!' said John. 'I'll make her a high coloratura. There are lots of old Queens of the Night looking for work!' The polar bear hunt stayed, but posterity has been denied exposure to my singing seagull and Husky Chorus!

In the year that followed, I had numerous trans-Atlantic phone calls from John, and dictated re-writes to him as requested. He wrote out Act One in full score and, during one of his trips to London, we used a room at the Royal Opera House for John to play through the score on the piano and sing all the parts. Going through the stage door at Covent Garden was a big thrill for me. I kept my eyes skinned for mega-stars, but they must have been having the afternoon off.

Then John began having doubts.

I re-worked the libretto while John worked on Act Two, with which he seemed to have fewer problems. When I heard his new music, it was clear at once that he was starting to think and compose visually, for the theatre rather than the concert platform. His first version of Act One was clearly deficient in this respect, although I didn't tell him this directly in case he lost confidence in the whole project. I was also concerned at the way he cut, edited and transposed my libretto, not always to its advantage, as I saw it. His first version of Act One seemed to have lost a lot and gained little.

In December 1988, I flew back to Banff, where the 'participants' (the word 'student' is avoided at Banff) had been preparing a workshop of Act Two. This taught John and me many things, and together we continued to work on sections of the libretto, challenging one another.

John was keen to have all the bits that would, literally, have been in Innuktitut, sung in that language. I thought that this made too much of the text impossibly obscure. In the spirit of the venture, we tried it, with the splendid help of Blendina, an Innuk translator.

At the presentation of the workshop, I told the story of the opera, while the singers performed the extracts that they had prepared. The result was received with enthusiastic curiosity by most of those present, although a Dene Indian thought the whole concept was racially exploitive (I disagree strongly). There were one or two dismissive voices, but a representative of the Edmonton Opera Company showed professional interest in the opera.

The truth is that so much of the score has yet to be written that it is impossible to be sure how the project will turn out. I have the conviction that *Tornrak* will be a popular success, if not a critical one. The story is exciting and full of visual incident. It should be good theatre. John is very committed to the piece now, and writing his best music. Whatever the outcome, *Tornrak* will not be boring. I believe Brian McMaster is of the same opinion, hence the advantage of the re-scheduling for 1990 and the adoption of *Tornrak* into the WNO's main touring repertoire.

My first duty as captain of the Haltwhistle Second Team was, sadly, to say a few words of appreciation about young Andrew Taylor and ask for a minute's silence in his memory. And so, on a grey afternoon at Humshaugh, by the North Tyne, in the shadow of Hadrian's Wall, we stood in two lines remembering poor Mouse.

May

Bob Douglas works for the Electricity Board. He came to read my meter. I asked him in for a coffee.

'I was once a prison officer. Back in 1969. I was twenty-four years old. I was told to stand by for C.C. Duty. That's Condemned Cell Duty. I was serving in Birmingham at the time. I was told to go to Bristol Prison to sit with Russell Pascoe. He'd just been condemned to death at Exeter Assizes. They used to get Prison Officers from outside the region for that sort of thing.'

Bob sipped his coffee, but declined a digestive biscuit. I said nothing, but waited for him to continue.

'I didn't actually know much about the case at first. I picked up my travel warrant and caught the train to Bristol. In my carriage there was someone reading the *Sunday Pictorial*. There was this lurid headline: 'I SHARED LOVE NEST WITH KILLERS.' Apparently, Russell Pascoe and Dennis Whitty, the other condemned man, had been living with two girls in a caravan. The men had been found guilty of murdering an old farmer during an attempted robbery.

'I was fixed up with bed and breakfast near Horfield Prison and started that night on the 10 pm to 7 am shift.'

'How many shifts were there?' I asked. Details like this can be difficult to research accurately.

'Three. 7 am to 2 pm, then 2 pm to 10 pm. We changed from one to another every week. There were no days off on C.C. Duty. Usually, the condemned cell was part of the main prison, but Horfield was different ... unique perhaps? It had its own condemned block and exercise yard.'

'A legacy from the Bloody Assizes?' I suggested.

'I'm not sure. Anyway, there were always two officers on duty at a time. I was paired with Ken, an ex-marine from Exeter Prison. Pascoe turned out to be a stocky young man of twenty-two. He had curly hair, I remember. We went in on the 3rd of November. Pascoe was due to be hanged on Tuesday the 19th of November.'

(I was silently surprised at Bob's precision with time and dates.)

'You see, condemned men were always allowed three clear Sundays, to make their peace with God. There was always an appeal, of course. If that was lost, a new date would be set.

'The cell was twenty-five feet long and twelve feet wide. At one end was Pascoe's bed, a cabinet and lamp. At the other was a table and three easy chairs. There was another lamp on the table. At nights, we would half cover it with a green cloth so we could read while Pascoe slept. There was a door leading to a bathroom, and another leading to the toilet. We had to be with him all the time. His pyjamas had ties, not buttons. Obviously there was no belt or neck-tie. Condemned men weren't allowed to harm themselves!

'There was another, locked door. It led across a narrow corridor to the Execution Chamber.

'To pass the time, there was a radio and various games, Monopoly, Scrabble, and playing cards. The Prison library changed the books once a week.'

'What did Pascoe read?'

'I can't remember. I think Ken and I did most of the reading. Pascoe had visits every day from the Governor, his Deputy or the Medical Officer. The Prison Chaplain was an ex-Royal Navy padre, who tried to teach Pascoe Bezique, which baffled the prisoner. At meal times, a relief officer brought Pascoe's meal to the cell. The officer relieved Ken and me, one at a time, so that we could go to the canteen to eat.

'Pascoe was allowed an hour's exercise a day. He seldom took the full hour. After thirty minutes, he was asking to go back inside. Then we took Pascoe to London for his appeal.'

'How did you travel?'

'By car to Pentonville. Then on to the Old Bailey. We had the same condemned cell as Crippen, Haig and Christie, actually. When we got back to our London lodgings that night, we heard about the Kennedy assassination, I remember.

'Pascoe lost his appeal. He petitioned the Home Secretary, Henry Brooke, then asked the Queen for clemency, both without success. His execution was set for 17th of December. The Press called them "The Christmas Hangings".'

'Did Pascoe tell you about the crime itself?'

'Yes. It's an odd story. The old farmer was a bit of a recluse. In 1917, he had deserted from the British Army and had hidden on his parents' farm until 1953! At the time of the Queen's Coronation, an amnesty was given to all deserters. Only then did the old man put in daytime appearances around the farm.

'Pascoe had done some farm work for him ... the old fellow was living alone by this time. Pascoe knew that he didn't bank his money. There was cash all over the place ... in drawers, behind books, under the mattress.

'One night, Pascoe and Whitty set out to rob him. They knocked on the farmhouse door and said they were part of a helicopter crew. They had been forced down and one of their mates had been injured! When the door was opened, Pascoe hit the farmer with an iron bar. Then Whitty pulled out a knife and stabbed the old man to death. Pascoe always said that he never knew Whitty had a knife. Killing the man was never part of the plan.'

'But Pascoe hit him over the head with an iron bar. That could have killed him,' I suggested.

'Anyway, on the 15th of December, Ken and I started our last stint with Pascoe. He was really down. He had no real interest in listening to the radio or playing cards any more. Outside the prison, anti-hanging demonstrators were protesting against "The Christmas Hangings".

'That evening, the Public Hangman, Harry Allen, and his assistant were in the Officers' Mess. Between hangings, Harry Allen was a Manchester publican. He had been chief assistant to Britain's most famous hangman, Albert Pierpoint for many years. Their services were in demand all over the Empire, not just in Britain.

'Allen had already been to see Pascoe. "Hello, son," he said, sticking out his hand to the prisoner, who shook it. The prisoner was also weighed and measured, so that Allen could calculate the precise distance of the drop. Too much rope, and Pascoe's head would be ripped off. Too little, and he might strangle. Allen was an artist.

'Then an odd thing happened. At about 10.30 pm on the eve of the execution, we heard the doors being unlocked. Pascoe's brother had arrived from Cornwall on the back of a motor scooter. The Chief allowed him in to say goodbye. What could they say to one another? It was sad. Ken and I broke it up after half an hour, to the relief of both of them.

'Pascoe took a sleeping draft, but lay on his bed, wide awake.

'Just before 7 am, Ken and I were relieved of our duty and went to the canteen. The last we saw of Pascoe, he was asleep. We never said goodbye.

'We had breakfast with Harry Allen and his assistant. At five minutes to eight, Allen got up and left the table. The Prison clock struck eight. On the fifth stroke, there was a clang as the trapdoor opened and bounced off the walls below.

'I suppose Pascoe was a bit unlucky. The following year, 1964, hanging was abolished. The last man to be hanged was in June of that year, at Strangeways, Manchester, actually.'

Two days later, I got a bill from the Electricity Board for £123.56.

I have now lived for more than three clear months without drinking alcohol! That's almost true. I have had a glass of sherry before Sunday lunch with John Clark at Featherstone Castle. But I have never got into the habit of going out to another pub after my enforced departure from The Wallace Arms.

I can report that although I did miss the habit of going out at six o'clock for an hour before supper at first, I no longer do. I have rediscovered the joys of the active evening, when what is left of my brain is not swimming or dozing. I can read and write when I wish, and with the extended hours of daylight this far north (you Southerners don't know what you're missing!), I can enjoy cricket 'nets' and evening games more than ever.

Some of you reading this may find it hard to swallow, but life without alcohol is a treat. If you don't believe me, I challenge you to try it.

Heavy beer-drinkers are spending an absurdly large proportion of their income on something that makes them slow, dozy and over-weight. At best, the beer addict becomes dully benign, at worst, given to bursts of irrational violence and social irresponsibility. The political consequences of this addiction include capitalistic control over a worker's income, and slavery to mind-numbing routine to provide enough regular cash to feed the habit. Addicts will regard this as nonsense, which proves my point, doesn't it?

Opera Now have just published the first of my articles. 'Recording the Drama' is about the problems that record producers face in trying to recreate theatrical drama in the recording studio. Unfortunately, one of the sub-editors has gone to work on what I submitted, and committed the unpardonable gaff of suggesting that King Marke has sailed to France at the end of Act One of *Tristan und Isolde*, instead of meeting Tristan's ship off the coast of Cornwall!

How trivial, you may think! Try telling that to all the thousands of opera queens who are chortling away at my expense!

So I've sent the following press release to Editor, Mel Cooper, who would rather receive something like this than an angry note, unless I have seriously misjudged him.

KING MARKE TAKES WRONG BOAT!
Furious rage of red faced King!

King Marke of Cornwall blamed *Opera Now* magazine for the recent fiasco in which he arrived in France to greet his new consort, Miss Isolde, when she had, in fact, been shipped to Cornwall by Sir Tristan, the young knight with whom King Marke's name was romantically linked in the gutter press some years ago.

French peasants fled in alarm at the unexpected approach of King Marke's armed ship, and they were only put at ease when the embarrassed King shared with them the elaborate picnic he had brought with him to impress his missing spouse-to-be.

It appears that the King is an avid reader of the new *Opera Now* magazine, and he had been led to believe that he should meet Miss Isolde in France as a result of an article by Michael Wilcox, the Devon born playwright who is now seeking sanctuary in the Kingdom of Northumbria. The King has graciously accepted Mr Wilcox's explanation, that the error occurred as a result of mischievous editing by someone at the *Opera Now* offices.

Opera Now editor, Mel Cooper, admits that the French fiasco was an in-house editorial blunder. Mr Cooper denies, however, that any of his staff are related to the Knight Melot, that traitor to Love.

A few days later, I got a good-natured reply card from Mel Cooper: 'I'll murder that Melot! He struck again this month on *Il Trovatore*!'

From now on, every editorial blunder at *Opera Now* will be blamed on Melot, betrayer of Tristan and Isolde.

May 1st 1974 was the day my contract with the Education Authority expired. From that moment onwards, I was a playwright, and I had my job description changed on my passport to prove it. What I had not done, however, was write a play!

During my time as Head of English at a Newcastle Comprehensive School, I had taken a particular interest in the activities of the Tyneside Theatre Company, run then by Gareth Morgan. This involved organising countless parties of students to the productions at the University Theatre (now called the Newcastle Playhouse), engaging the Touring Company, Stagecoach, as often as possible to come and perform at the school, and generally publicising all events associated with the theatre. Before long, whenever boys or girls were needed in any of the Main House productions, the theatre turned to me to seek volunteers for the auditions. For a while in 1973, every new production (there was one every three or four weeks!) had a group of my students in it. This, in turn, encouraged many more young people to come to the productions. The seat sales that my enthusiasm created became economically significant.

At the same time, as soon as my official school day was finished, I was busy with the Northumberland Experimental Youth Theatre, helping, as requested, with the latest C. P. Taylor

1a My father,
Denys Wilcox.

1b My family in 1951.
Left to right:
John, me, Mark and my mother, Sally.

2a Aged fifteen.

2b C.P. Taylor.

3a Jean Anderson and Patience Collier in *Lent* at the Lyric Hammersmith Studio, February 1983.

3b The BBC television production of *Lent* in February 1985.
From left to right: Constance Chapman, David Langton, Fabia Drake, Graham McGrath, Harry Andrews.

4 Stevan Rimkus and Douglas Sannachan in *Rents* at the Lyric Hammersmith in February 1984.

5a Dexter Fletcher as Rikki in *Massage* at the Lyric Hammersmith Studio in November 1986.

5b John Thaw (centre) as Inspector Morse, flanked by Kevin Whatley (left) and Terence Hardiman in *Last Bus to Woodstock* for Zenith/Central Television.

6 Penelope Walker as Milak
in the Welsh National Opera's
production of *Tornrak* in May 1990.

7 David Owen as Arthur
with Penelope Walker
in *Tornrak*.

8a The Haltwhistle Second XI in 1989. *Back row, left to right*: John Archibald, Graham Lee, Paul Dancer, John Hepple, Chris Anson, Ian Archibald. *Front row, left to right*: Chris Smith, Eddie Howe, Michael Wilcox (captain), Tom Lee, Steven Pape.

8b A lucky bottom edge for four!

production. At that time, Cecil Taylor was one of the most prolific playwrights in the country, writing for The Traverse Theatre, Edinburgh, The Tyneside Theatre Company, Live Theatre, Newcastle and later for the Oxford Playhouse, and the Royal Shakespeare Company.

This Russian Jew from Glasgow had been politically active at least from the 1950s. I believe he used his initials C. P. rather than the customary forename because of its association with the Communist Party. He boasted of being an anarchist, if encouraged, although the most anarchic thing about him was the shambles of the shed in his garden, in which he demolished a succession of typewriters. Cecil saw it as part of his political work to encourage and teach new playwrights, and long before I had written my first play, I had got to know him and his family well. When I told him that I was giving up teaching to start a career as a writer and that his influence was partly responsible for my change of direction, he looked pleased and puzzled and said, 'You're daft, Wilcox! You know that?'

Once freed from the routine of school life, I spent a couple of weeks in the Newcastle Central Library, sitting amongst the students who were preparing for their examinations, and writing in long hand *Dekka and Dava* (now published by Methuen in *'Massage' and other plays*).

After completing a draft of *Dekka and Dava* in biro, I went off and bought a second-hand typewriter on which I typed a second draft with two fingers. Cecil was surprised by the play and thought it showed promise. As a result of his enthusiasm, Gareth Morgan asked me if I would write an hour-long play for the Stagecoach Company. He offered me £100, which I gratefully accepted. My professional career was underway!

And Newcastle was an excellent place to be based. During the '74–75 season, the Tyneside Theatre Company's productions included *Cyrano de Bergerac* in an adaptation by James Kirkup, Shaw's *Widowers' Houses* and *Woyzeck*, directed by Keith Hack and with a cast that included Richard Griffiths, Ron Cook, Jonathan Kent, Patti Love, Ian McDiarmid and Barry Stanton (music by Stephen Oliver). In addition, there was a play about George Stephenson and the birth of the Railway, *All Change*, co-scripted by Richard Cooper and C. P. Taylor, a Stagecoach production of Barry Reckord's *Skyvers* which caused a scandal with its challenge to authority in schools and realistic language, and two further Stagecoach productions that I scripted, the most interesting of which (although terminally flawed) was about the history of the Atomic Bomb.

Other professional companies in Newcastle at this time included Live Theatre, Bruvvers and Skin and Bones, each of which had its own personality and political stance. I took an interest in all of them, and just seeing all the work that was going on, and following a production from rehearsals to performances in various venues in the region was both instructive and time consuming.

Meanwhile, Cecil and I, with other playwrights in the North East, set up Northern Playwrights' Society to promote the interests of playwrights living and working in the Northern Arts region. I was elected secretary with an open mandate to get on with things and to report back to the other members once a month. This gave me access to all those involved in theatre and new writing.

Particular achievements of Northern Playwrights' Society included its own standard form of contract, which retained control of residual rights in the hands of the playwright, an association with a local publisher, Iron Press, which resulted in a series of North East plays being published, and the setting up of the Northern Drama Library at the Newcastle Central Library.

This was a scheme whereby all plays written in the region, regardless of merit, were photocopied and placed in the archives and on special access shelves as an independent collection. The advantages of this were that there was no selection panel, deciding what should or should not be included. (Who are we to say what might be of interest in a hundred years time?) Secondly, playwrights were forced to study their manuscripts carefully and prepare an approved draft for copying.

You may think that a playwright knows what the text of his or her play is, but the truth is that after a first production, there are likely to be many textural changes to the script with which the company started rehearsals. Sometimes the playwright will want to incorporate these changes into the text, but sometimes changes are made to suit particular actors and productions, and the playwright might want to revert to the original text. Sometimes wholesale re-writing is necessary. The temptation after a production of a new play is for the bits and pieces of script to be stuffed into a folder and stuck on a shelf. Only if the script is wanted for publication, or, in the case of the Northern Drama Library, for photocopying, is the playwright likely to get the text into proper order.

C. P. Taylor had bits of plays all over his shed, and he spent much time in reassembling them before presenting them to me for copying. As a result, most of Cecil's unpublished work is stored at the Newcastle Central Library in drafts prepared by him that I photocopied. The collection also includes manuscripts by Sid Chaplin, Len Barras, Tom Haddaway, Phil Woods, Kate Collingwood and many others. Setting up this scheme, which still operates today, was the most important innovation of my five years as NPS secretary.

Cecil was intensely curious about everything. Give him a pile of books (we often swapped and discussed our current reading) and he gutted them for information with unbelievable speed. I am a slow and precise reader, which means that when I read a book, it really has been read, every word. Cecil was the opposite. He skimmed and scavenged a text. You always knew when he had read a book by its tattered, exhausted condition. It was the same with scripts. I would show him something I had been working on for the past few weeks and he would glance rapidly at page after page and then thrust it back at me, sometimes with approval, but often with a dismissive remark. If he paused to study a page carefully, you knew he had come across something worthwhile.

Driving him up to rehearsals at the Traverse in Edinburgh was further education for me. The reputations of leading directors were more than tarnished in his dismissive tirades. He was far more appreciative of the talents of actors. The truth was that there were very few directors with whom he could establish a successful working relationship. Cecil was prolific in his script writing to a fault. What he needed help with was organising his material. He wanted to be challenged. He was never much in control of the overall structure of a play, and even his dialogue needed stern editing. He was always inclined to over use expletives and colloquial expressions. He worked straight onto his manual typewriters and rather than sit doing nothing would fill the page full of dots whenever he paused.

And yet ... and yet ... Cecil was a great writer. He had an individual vision of the world about him and tackled with rare courage the toughest subjects. His last completed play was *Good*, which was produced to memorable effect by the Royal Shakespeare Company in London and New York. It tells the story of how a seemingly benign academic shared responsibility for the murder of millions in the Nazi extermination camps.

Cecil returned home from London as the play opened (September 1981). He was exhausted, taken to hospital and died. I am not alone in believing that with better medical attention, he would still be alive today.

With a cruel irony, the *Guardian* had announced his new play thus: 'GOOD-BYE, C. P. TAYLOR'.

May has been blessed with endless, warm sunshine. The garden has loved it and so have I. Curlews, plovers, oyster-catchers and a gooseander are all nesting nearby and my garden is full of wrens, robins, swallows and blue-tits, and pied wagtails.

And the cricket pitches have been hard and good for batting! So far we have won six matches and lost two. We might have won the lot if our two opening bowlers had not injured themselves at the same time. Steven Pape got sat on playing football and wrecked his ribs and a knee, while 'Bona' Hepple fell on his shoulder while attempting a catch, and had to be taken to hospital! Our new, seventeen-year-old wicket keeper, Chris Smith, is doing excellently, and the Junior captain, Graham Lee, has been opening our batting with a sound defence, but without much attack. Part of my role as captain is to give these fine young players a chance to develop their talents. I do this by giving them responsibility and every encouragement.

An additional pleasure has been acting as driver and umpire for the Haltwhistle juniors. They play eighteen six-ball overs in the evenings. The games are taken quite seriously, but with good humour. Amusing incidents (people bumping into one another, dropped 'skyers', chaotic run outs) are greeted with roars of approval by both sides, but never with cruelty. The older boys of both sides see that the youngsters, who are sometimes very small, are not put at risk. A fast bowler (and sixteen-year-olds can be quick) bowls half pace at a young tail-ender without having to be told.

After the self-centred aggression that marked out the boys of my own childhood, I find this natural generosity of spirit most touching. It made an immediate impression on me when I first travelled north, twenty-five years ago. In the world from which I had come, boys called all adults 'Sir', 'Miss' or 'Mrs' and it came as a culture shock to hear adults addressed by their Christian names or nick-names by even the youngest children. In my former world, people were trained from the cradle to trample over each other to get power and position. If that involved stifling talent, and putting people down with all manner of emotional and physical pressure, so be it. But on arrival in this Northern land, with its distinct dialects and vocabulary, its different history and stable, inter-married communities, I found people wanted to see the best in one another. Young and old were bonded by affection and good will, rather than aggression and selfishness.

And twenty-five years on, even after ten years of Thatcherism, which has exploited that same selfishness and aggression with relentless dedication, the best in people is still thriving up here amongst my young friends on the cricket field and the Young Farmers' Club, and my older friends in the town.

In fairness, I had better report one unfortunate incident concerning an evening knockout match with Humshaugh (sixteen eight-ball overs). We arrived, correctly, at their ground at six o'clock. In error, they travelled to our ground at Haltwhistle. By the time they had realised their mistake, it was past seven o'clock and some of their team had gone missing. It had been raining and the ground was wet, but hard underneath. No wicket was cut or marked out. We would have gratefully accepted the match had it been offered to us, but were prepared to play on the previous Saturday's wicket, whose markings were still just about visible. Humshaugh obviously didn't fancy playing us with only eight men and saved their skins by declaring their ground closed and unfit for play!

My team was furious, but the 'Halty' lads kept their heads. Border wars have started with less provocation in the past! We had to return to Humshaugh the following Monday for the replay, which we won. But do you think such mischief will be forgotten? No chance!

The Wallace Arms is up for sale.

In the past fifteen years, I have worked with many different theatre directors, including Jan Sargent, Ian Forrest, Chris Parr, Peter Lichtenfels, Christopher Fettes and William ('Bill') Gaskill. In most cases, they were directing a new play of mine that was receiving its première performance. Chris Parr directed the première of *Rents*, Peter Lichtenfels was responsible for the first productions of *Accounts* and *78 Revolutions*, and Christopher Fettes was the first director of *Lent*. Bill Gaskill directed a revival of *Rents* at the Lyric, Hammersmith.

Each had a different attitude towards the new script, and each treated the playwright differently. Chris Parr specialised in directing new plays and was an outstandingly successful artistic director of the Traverse Theatre, Edinburgh, where I first encountered him. Chris challenged every word of the script, suggesting all sorts of re-writes. This can be confusing for an inexperienced writer. I was in awe of all the seasoned professionals around me, giving advice, and it was difficult to decide how to react. For better or worse, the playwright must finally make up his or her own mind about what the text should be. There are times when bad ideas can be forced on a writer and it is then best to stand your ground. I now listen to each challenge and try to decide whether it is a script problem, an actor problem, or a director problem and react accordingly.

At the Traverse, as elsewhere, I was restricted to a small cast for economic reasons, but at Chris Parr's suggestion, I wrote a series of scenes that showed the two 'rent boys' with various 'punters'. 'I think we can run to an extra actor if you write the scenes well enough,' he told me. I wrote all the punter scenes at a sitting one morning, and slotted them into the script. The punters were mostly based on characters I had encountered in the Newcastle City Baths Sauna, or Newcastle's sleazy Gay nightclub, which in those days was Club Maris on the Westgate Road. (If you think that's an odd name for a nightclub, it was called Mario's, but when a local Italian restaurant complained, someone went out with a hammer and knocked the 'O' and the apostrophe off the wall, leaving 'Maris'!)

After working on the script with the playwright over a protracted period of time, Chris Parr then required the writer to stay in rehearsals for at least a week, so the actors could challenge the script and ideas could fly around freely. Instant re-writes were not uncommon. The Traverse had a 'rehearsal attendance allowance' for the playwright to cover additional expenses during this process. Then, for the last week of rehearsals, I was allowed time to myself while the company got on with the job.

How different this experience was to working with Christopher Fettes on *Lent*! I read the whole script to him in his house one afternoon. He sat listening without making any comments. When I finished, he carried on sitting there, silently.

'Is it OK?' I ventured, cautiously.

'Yes,' he said.

'Do you want any re-writes?'

'No.'

I was never asked to any of the auditions. I gather there were many for the part of the twelve-year-old Paul, including the young Sam West, son of Timothy West and Prunella Scales, who has become one of the most in demand actors of his generation. Eventually, Christopher Fettes cast Jonathan Kent, an actor of about my age, in the part, rather than a boy as the text required. Presumably, that was one of the things he was considering when he asked me to read through the script. This device of an older man reliving his youth did work, but having a boy would have been so much better. And since this was the first production of the play, and not a revival, I believe that there was an obligation to attempt to direct the play as intended. Excellent though Jonathan Kent was, casting him was a cop out by the director. And the knowledge that we might have had young Sam West still haunts me.

After the read-through, with a cast that also included Patience Collier, Wensley Pithey, Dennis Edwards and Jean Anderson, I was told I wasn't wanted for rehearsals and found myself out on the streets! This was not because I was a difficult or interfering person. I think Christopher Fettes was used to directing the work of dead playwrights and was confused at having a live one around the place. Later, I did attend one or two rehearsals, but I never got to know the director or the cast particularly well, and was made to feel like an uninvited guest. However, the production and the individual performances were memorable, and Christopher Fettes proved an inspired and original director.

Peter Lichtenfels took over the Traverse Theatre when Chris Parr moved into television. In both *Accounts* and *78 Revolutions* Peter adopted the Chris Parr working method of involving the playwright in the first ten days of rehearsals. Peter is almost too kind to the writer, and if he had challenged the script of *78 Revolutions* harder, it might have been a better play. All the pre-production work on *Accounts* was done by Chris Parr, not Peter, and Chris certainly made major contributions to its development, although Peter, quite deservedly, took the credit for its successful first production, which transferred him from the Traverse to the Riverside Studios, Hammersmith.

Peter is very much a playwright's director, taking the greatest trouble to ensure that the writer has somewhere decent to stay during rehearsals and feels completely involved in the production. This is rare. Too many directors make even the best behaved playwright feel like an intruder. If the play is a success, this type of director likes to hog all the credit, pushing the writer as far out of sight as possible.

This is especially true of revivals. For a year or two, in pre-AIDS Britain, there were numerous productions of *Rents*, all of which I saw. On some occasions, I was introduced to the cast and invited out after the performance, whilst on others, I was lucky to be offered a drink in the bar. It seems that when a play has taken off (however brief the flight) the playwright becomes a name on a programme, a shadow at the back of the stalls.

Working with Bill Gaskill (whose autobiographical account of his time at The Royal Court Theatre, *A Sense of Direction*, Faber 1988, I recommend enthusiastically) on the Lyric Hammersmith revival of *Rents* was a pleasure from beginning to end. Bill took the greatest care with the casting (it was especially difficult finding the right Robert), and during rehearsals, which I was free to attend, or not, as I wished, Bill developed a marvellous relationship with the company, stopping the action from time to time and asking specific questions about the precise meaning of lines and what was going on at that moment. He was both firm and gentle and we all loved him. He didn't offer solutions or short cuts to the actors, preferring them to analyse problems for themselves and test out various performing options. By working through questions rather than dictates, he drew the company more deeply into the drama. In this production, the actors were never mere puppets of the director.

Any playwright having a new script in production for the first time should make sure that, by the time of the read-through, the script is as thoroughly written as possible. It is not fair on the company to do too much re-writing during rehearsals. There are usually only three weeks between the company assembling for the first time to the first public preview, and the actors will want to be rehearsing 'off the book' by the middle of the second week. It is therefore vital that writer and director work through the script well before rehearsals start.

Secondly, the playwright has a special role in trying to get the very best out of the actors, director, designer, the house staff of the theatre and other interested parties. In rehearsals, challenges to an untried script can be fierce. It is difficult for an inexperienced playwright to distinguish between a script problem and an actor or director problem. Directors working with a new writer should remember this. The temptation for an insecure writer is to defend the script at all costs, whereas in fact the challenges of actors are often most useful in sharpening focus. Actors have an important role in shaping a new script. The ability to distinguish between good and bad ideas is an important, but not easy, skill for a playwright to develop.

Too often, a script that looks good on the page, and reads well enough, will not play well in production. Scripts are not written to be read, they are written for performance, which is a totally different thing. A problem that I have encountered, especially working for television, is that producers and directors cannot distinguish between a script that reads efficiently and one that will play well. The costs of making television film dramas is such that there is minimal rehearsal before each scene is shot, and the script has to work first time. Producers can show signs of panic at a lean-looking script, often wanting more dialogue than is necessary. Sometimes I have to assure the producer that the script will, indeed, work. Trust me! Trust the writer! Please!

In the theatre, the playwright has more time to get to know everybody. It is both interesting in its own right, and important for the production, to arouse curiosity and enthusiasm for the new work in hand. While the director and the cast are hard at work, the playwright has time to make personal contact with everyone at the theatre. The writer is also useful to the publicity department as one of the few people around able to talk about the new play with confidence. So playing a friendly role around the place, without getting knee deep in the internal politics of the theatre is an important part of the playwright's responsibilities.

I have been working on a new draft of *Special*, the film script that BBC Scotland commissioned, and then rejected, a couple of years ago. Maybe, Michael Darlow, who directed *Accounts* for Film on Four will be interested? Tyne Tees Television have joined Scottish Television in telling me *Special* is no good, but I don't believe any of them!

In the new draft, I have developed the sombre theme of suicide in the country (alarmingly common) and its effect on those who are left behind. Because this script was conceived from the start as a film, rather than a stage play, I have made it full of visual opportunities of the sort that American film makers thrive on, but which seem to leave British TV producers, with their dependence on dialogue rather than pictures, floundering.

The idea for *Special* came from the attempt by an enthusiastic local policeman to set up groups of Special constables in the valley. Policing in the country is quite different from urban policing. In the country, everyone knows everyone else, who owns each car, motor bike and bicycle. If anything out of the ordinary occurs, someone is bound to notice. The country, to an outsider, may look private and deserted, but it has eyes and ears quite foreign to the city. Most police come from urban backgrounds and it takes time for them to understand what the hell is going on out here.

In my story, a solitary eccentric, 'Manky' Morris, is recruited as a 'Special'. His uniform and new authority get the better of him and he starts to betray the minor misdemeanours of his neighbours to the new and over zealous sergeant, with catastrophic consequences. What seems to be working against my script is that it is rural, rather than urban (surely a plus?) and that so much of it is visual rather than dialogue based. This hits at British television drama where it is at its weakest. Telling stories through moving images rather than theatrical dialogue sends most television directors and producers running for cover. What they cannot hear from the printed page doesn't seem to exist. Film, unlike traditional British theatre, is visual, not verbal. But try explaining that to your over paid and comfortable British TV producer and he (they are mostly male) will show you the door.

June

My five years at Malvern College, a Public School in Elgar country on the Malvern Hills seem far less real than my young life that preceded them. Did they really happen? Were they in this life or were they part of an earlier existence? I had asked my mother to send me to drama school, if I had to be sent away from home, rather than to Malvern. 'You'll have it knocked out of you at Public School,' vengeful teachers used to mutter. *Tom Brown's Schooldays* and *Stalky and Co* were still held up to us in the 1950s as honourable examples of Public School life. Fagging, beatings and roastings didn't seem much fun to me, but that was my ordained path and no amount of pleading was going to change my mother's mind. 'It's what Daddy would have wanted,' she said with a sigh.

I did 'fag' for two years. I was beaten a couple of times by older boys with gym shoes for talking after lights-out, but I'm not aware that anyone was roasted, Tom Brown fashion. Most of the teachers were decent old plodders at their chosen profession. If it wasn't for their older appearance, I doubt if you could have picked most of them out from the crowd of boys they were trying to teach. And like the boys, most were aggressively disinterested in the arts. The few who were more positively inclined still seemed to find anything from the twentieth century both difficult and culturally dangerous.

Our greatly respected history master, Ralph Blumeneau, presented Vaughan Williams's 'Fantasia on a theme of Thomas Tallis' to us as a tough nut that he had recently cracked. He then played us a recording of Walton's 'Belshazzar's Feast' with an anarchic gleam in his eye. That such period pieces, decades old and so instantly accessible, should be presented to us as the new and the daring seems now to be symptomatic of the cultural timidity of that isolated world. To his further credit, Ralph Blumeneau transformed his classroom into an art gallery, changing the reproductions, neatly framed in uniform size, every few weeks. He would talk to us about the artist thus represented and encourage us to discuss our reactions to what we saw. Unremarkable, are you thinking? In the late fifties, teachers who showed such enthusiasm seemed rare indeed to us.

Thatcherism, which has consistently undervalued the arts and done its best to snuff out anything socially or politically challenging has its roots in the attitudes of Public Schools of the fifties. There was both fear of the new, and a lack of confidence to explore, challenge, and debate the old, or show enthusiasm for anything that had not already been granted a seal of approval, that stunted and frustrated our curiosity. Those introductions to twentieth-century composers and artists, done with a sense of guilty daring that may seem extraordinary today, were moments of crucial importance in my life.

Thanks are also due to Mr Russell, who only survived briefly at Malvern, for introducing me to recordings of Fedor Chaliapin singing *Boris Godunov* live at Covent Garden in 1928, and for lending me his mono set of Decca's now historic recording of *Das Rheingold*. The encounter with each opened further doors and changed the direction of my life. As I listened to Chaliapin through a cobweb of crackles, I thought I was in the presence of Godunov himself. There was the ghost of the murdered boy (me, in my imagination) returning to haunt the guilty Tsar and drive him to insanity. My interest in 'classical' music (that absurdly inaccurate logo) set me apart from my immediate peers, and it was only in my fifth year at Malvern that I found some like-minded enthusiasts spread thinly around the nine other Houses at the school.

On a few occasions I lugged my portable record player up to a deserted classroom for an evening recital, extending an open invitation to anyone interested. Choosing Richard Strauss's 'Death and Transfiguration' as one of the concert items, I plotted out a moment by moment synopsis of the piece with a stop watch and wrote out the programme on the blackboard. Six or seven boys attended, and, to my surprise, one master, 'Gus' Surtees, all risking the scorn of the mob.

Many books have been written about Public School life, and all that I have read have contained enough truth to give me nightmares. Lindsay Anderson's film *If...* captured the institutionalised aggression, the power structure of privilege and the homoeroticism of single sex boarding schools with alarming accuracy.

Part of the social structure of Malvern was built around the privileges that depended on how long you had been at the school. From memory, these included walking around with one hand in a jacket pocket after one term, two hands in jacket pockets after two terms, one hand in a trouser pocket after one year, both hands in trousers pockets after two, the middle button of your black jacket could be left undone after ... was it three years? Tie pins, patterned socks, a carnation in your jacket buttonhole on Speech Day, and a host of other trivia all came into the scheme of things.

If this list seems quaint (and contravention led to various punishments, including being 'nipped off' in which the unfortunate victim lost all his privileges for a week or two) other rules were more sinister. A boy was not allowed to talk to another boy more than four terms his senior. This was expressly to prevent romantic liasons, affection between consenting humans of either sex being considered morally dangerous.

For the first two years, twelve of us shared the 'end study' at No. 3 House, and, like it or not, had to get on with each other as best we could.

Soon, some of those mysterious facts of life that had eluded my comprehension were revealed. A boy called Hoskins staggered in all bleary eyed after breakfast and announced that he had had a marvellous wank the night before.

'A marvellous what?' I asked, innocently.

'Wank! Flog! Rub up!' he exclaimed mischievously, with graphic hand movements.

I was struck dumb. What could he be talking about?

The other boys came tumbling into the study, chattering, collecting books for the morning's lessons.

I went over to Hoskins.

'I don't understand,' I whispered.

'You rub yourself and white stuff comes out. Go and try it.'

I left the study, jumped downstairs two at a time, ran across the yard to the outside lavatories and locked myself in a cubicle. To my complete astonishment, I found out that what Hoskins had told me was true!

'Hurry up in there!'

'For Christ's sake hurry up!'

'It's chapel in two minutes!'

I tried to clean myself up with horrid, non-absorbent bog-roll, wondering what on earth I'd done and what it meant, and was it a sin, and everybody would know as soon as they saw me, and Oh God! There's the chapel bell!

'Look! I'm crapping in my pants, you little oik!'

Thump! Thump! On the bog door.

I emerged.

'Sorry . . .' I said, and ran from the scene of my new and addictive crime.

June is tremendously hot! We had a special cricket match on the sixth, my birthday, down at Featherstone Castle. Some of the lads from Allendale came over. They were far too good for the Featherstone team, who used the match as practice, and I was quietly delighted by the way they entered into the spirit of things by not bowling too fast or taking advantage of their superior skills. After a happy game, with lots of good humour, we had refreshments and gossip in the Castle.

'Trouble is,' says Steven Chalton, 'the show committee is charging us the earth for our pitch.'

'Aye,' says Sandy, 'they've got us over a barrel.'

'There's no other flat ground around. Only the show ground.'
'All the money we raise goes on paying the ground rent, not on improving things,' says Ali.
'And they're all rich farmers!'
'Can't you get back at them?' I suggest.
'How?'
'Well, tell them if it wasn't for the good work the Cricket Club does, the place would be over-run by hoodlums!'
'It is already . . .'
'They're o'er greedy. That's the top and bottom of it, Michael.'
'Oh dear, let me think . . .'
'We've all had a good think about it.'
'Why not check out the title deeds to the show ground and see exactly who owns it and what their rights are.'
'We know all about that. It's no good.'
'Just have to stick to poaching the buggers' pheasants!'
'That's it! Organise a mass poach of all the farmers on the Show Committee, sell all the deer, the pheasants, the salmon, and give the money back to the farmers as rent!'
'Done that for years.'
'Michael, would you be interested in being a Vice President of the club?' asks Steven.
'Well, what an honour! Of course I would, if asked.'
'It'll cost you, mind,' adds Sandy.
'No, it won't, Michael,' says Steven.
'I'd be delighted to be a Vice President and make a contribution to the club each year.'
'Right,' says Steven, 'I'll bring it up at the next Committee meeting.'

How pleasant it is to get up in the morning, then not have to go into work. Who wants to work anyway? The sun is shining. The garden is alive with nesting birds. The grass needs cutting and the hedges trimming. The strawberries are coming on and the fruit needs raising off the ground. I must sow some more radishes and set the broad beans going. And there's a week's washing to do. Perfect weather for drying clothes on the line.

Not much chance of work today! Or tomorrow. Or the next day! If the weather keeps up the way it is.

And that is the problem! Unless I am under the cosh to complete a script, or an article, or a book even, by a stern deadline, this writer (like most others, I guess) has a thousand excuses for doing everything except write.

So what's to be done?

Firstly, I have a regime under which I manage to write and do all the other things I'd rather be doing. This involves getting out of bed in the morning, making a pot of tea and going directly into my study to write for a couple of hours before breakfast. If I turn on the record player, my soul is lost! I cannot work and listen to music. Music demands my full attention. Visitors who come to my house, ask to listen to my hi-fi system, then chatter while the music is playing, get a zero rating from me! (Along with those who see my old, black oven range and immediately ask if I bake my own bread.)

After that initial writing session, I eat breakfast, then return for session two. If the telephone goes, I answer it, but never talk for long. If the caller gets off the main purpose of the call, I am abrupt. If I have to call someone, I start off saying, 'Briefly ...' and get on with it like a spoken telegram. Time is too precious to waste. My regular callers understand the rules and are relieved not to make small talk. This means that people can call me if they need to and know that there is no chatter.

After four hours of writing, the time is around eleven or half past and I spend the rest of the morning shopping for food and a newspaper (*Guardian* or *Independent* mid-week, *Times* on a Saturday. *The Sunday Times* is delivered to my door for a 2p surcharge.)

My post arrives any time between ten o'clock and twelve-thirty, depending on which postman is on duty. There is no second delivery in the country.

The rest of the day is spent reading, walking, listening to music, cooking and watching television through till midnight.

Once (sometimes twice) a week, I go into Newcastle to hunt for compact disc bargains and take a trip to the sauna or turkish bath (depending on the day), for which there is a great social tradition in the North East. I like to think that this is a legacy from the days of the Roman occupation, but it is more likely that the dying industries of coal mining and ship building have more to do with it. Unlike some London saunas I could name, where the clients drift around like silent waifs, up here people talk and socialise, discuss present issues, sort out crossword puzzles, want to know your business and generally show a good-natured respect for young and old alike.

Nakedness is a social leveller. So the judge can sweat it out with the prisoner on bail, the professor with his student, rich man, poor man, beggar man, thief – all can hang up their outward identities for a couple of hours and converse, sleep, or flirt even, as the mood takes them. As well as its intended pleasures, there is also, for me, the opportunity to listen and observe a constantly changing diversity of characters, which, in turn, gives me something to write about in the mornings.

As editor of Methuen's *Gay Plays* anthologies, I have been reading scripts from around the world since 1983. *Volume Four* is due to go to press at the end of August, so it is decision time once again. In the running are plays by Eric Bentley (*Round Two*), Gerald Killingworth (*Days of Cavafy*), and Robert Patrick (*Let me not mar that perfect dream*), while I am continuing to try and track down a copy of Julian Green's *South*. Other interesting scripts have been received from Alex Harding in Australia (*Only Heaven Knows*), Ken Sofronski in New York (*I Played the Palace*) and French dramatist Jean Marie Besset (*The Function*).

Part of anthology building is concerned with finding the right mix of plays for each volume. I like to unearth a play long out of print that I can juxtapose with contemporary work. J. R. Ackerley's *The Prisoners of War* and Mordaunt Shairp's *The Green Bay Tree* have served this purpose, and *South* might still do for the latest publication. I also like to have plays from different parts of the world in each volume, which has meant Britain and America so far.

I am keeping an interested eye on a play by Isherwood and Bacardy, the work of British actor/writer Neil Bartlett, and hope that the re-write of Anthony Davison's *Screamers*, due for a new production at the Arts Theatre in London, will show more muscle and a better structure than the earlier draft I read.

I have also been to see actors Richard O'Callaghan and Elizabeth Quinn, who have a house in Godalming, Surrey. Elizabeth, who is profoundly deaf, had a huge international success with *Children of a Lesser God* a few years ago. Since then, she has done a limited amount of work. When I met Richard during the shooting of the first BMA video, I asked if he and Elizabeth would like me to have a go at writing a piece for them both to appear in, and this month's meeting is the result.

Elizabeth Quinn is one of those rare people that everyone loves at first sight. I was keenly interested to hear what her voice sounded like. Astonishingly, her sense of pitch is natural and expressive. How someone who has never heard the human voice, as a hearing person experiences it, and who has never heard a note of music, or the birds sing, or the daily noises that most of us take for granted, can pitch speech so perfectly is a miracle. However, I did notice that not all her pronunciation of words (I mean clear consonants and accurate vowel sounds) sounded entirely natural. Maybe the fact that she is American and is midway into speaking with a British accent (another mystery that such a transition should occur in a profoundly deaf person) has something to do with it. Nevertheless, I could see no reason why I should not write a part for Elizabeth in which her deafness plays no part. I was delighted to hear that there is talk of her playing the lead in *Hedda Gabler* in London later this year.

Before driving me to Godalming, Richard, who is playing one of the leads in David Hare's new play, *The Secret Rapture*, at the National Theatre, read some poems by young finalists in the W. H. Smith's Young Poets competition. A young Geordie lad brought the house down with his rendering of a poem in North

East dialect. Another boy was really upset that the award would be reported in his local newspaper.

'They'll think I'm a wimp!' he murmured, almost in tears.

'Who?'

'My mates.'

'No they won't,' I said. 'They'll be proud of you.'

'They'll think I'm soft.'

'For writing a poem?'

'Yes.'

'Are you a wimp?'

'No!'

'Well! There you are, then! Nothing to worry about.'

During the same few days in London, I had a useful half hour with Antony Peattie at the *Opera Now* offices in Grape Street. Antony has promised me some more opera recordings to review, starting with CD reissues of Britten's *Billy Budd*, *Albert Herring* and *Curlew River*. These will be followed by Sinopoli's new *Tannhauser* (with Domingo), operas by Respighi and another new *Tosca*. (Who this time?)

Overshadowing all this was the appalling news coming out of China. The democracy movement, encamped in Tiananmen Square, with The Goddess of Democracy a crude but potent icon, was suddenly overrun by the so-called People's Army. In full view of the world's television cameras, hundreds of people have been massacred and their bodies reduced to pulp by tanks. Others are being hunted down and executed.

One of my neighbouring farmers, Andy, is in the habit of wearing a People's Army badge in his cap. While out on one of my walks, I stopped to chat.

'Why are you still wearing that badge? Haven't you seen the television?'

He hadn't heard the news. I told him what I'd seen, hours before. The next time we met, there was no badge in his blue beret.

Meanwhile, who should be caught up in the brutality in China than Geraldine Easter, with whom I stay during my London visits.

She is over there, doing research for her forthcoming expedition and film about the 'Wild Man'.

News came through, at last, that Geraldine was safe, although she was one of the last Brits to get out. Her secretary here, Bernadette Drury, had done a splendid job, guessing which airport Geraldine might get to and booking a seat in an aircraft that she might try to catch. Astonishingly, Geraldine arrived at the right airport, somewhere in the South of China, to discover that she was booked on the next flight out by her trusty saviour in London! Well done, Bernadette! But my plans to go to China and direct a production of *Lent* look even more distant now.

Then the long journey home for me. Three and a half hours to Newcastle, then an hour's wait at the station, then another hour to Haltwhistle, then an hour's walk to my house. I arrive home with relief that everything is how I left it, but also an emptiness that there is no one there to say welcome. My stupid fault!

Even at thirteen, I knew there was something profoundly wrong with Malvern, but my experience of life had been so sheltered (and would remain so for many years) that it was difficult to articulate the wrongness or to challenge it. Elitism and privilege were fundamental to the place, but not merely in the arcane ways already described. We were special, we were repeatedly told. We were to be the leaders of industry, the professionals, doctors, lawyers, soldiers of Christ (as revealed to the Church of England, of course) and Queen and country. Other young people who lived in the nearby town of Great Malvern, but who went to local State schools, were not to be fraternised with, and were known as 'oiks'. Indeed, special permission had to be given for trips into town, and since the school had its own general store, there was seldom need to leave hallowed ground, except for walks on the hills and the regular cross country runs.

'The greatest disasters of the twentieth century are Freud, Stravinsky and D. H. Lawrence!' I was told, two World Wars not withstanding. The choral society, in which, with my natural tenor voice, I shyly sang the bass line in everything, performed Mendelssohn's *Elijah*. 'Take all the prophets of Baal, and let not one of them escape us! Take all and slay them!' we yelled with fundamentalist zeal. Then *Messiah*. 'Lord of Lords and King of Kings,' we thundered. And the *German Requiem* of Brahms, which aroused some political controversy, being considered a little too German. The headmaster had to declare publicly that the Brahms was a special favourite of his and how much he was looking forward to the performance, to quell rebellion in the ranks. On the day, the hapless soprano, bussed in for the occasion, hardly got a note right in her lovely solo, so all the scorn that had been building up for weeks was dumped on her. 'Bloody women!' muttered the Chaplain.

In the library, there was a great row about whether we should be allowed to read William Golding's recent novel, *Lord of the Flies*. In spite of substantial lobbying by some members of staff (and, astonishingly, some senior boys!), the dreaded book was finally cleared. I was reading Zola's *Germinal* at the time, which had been on the library shelves so long, and was so unread, that the zealots were evidently unaware of the dynamite that lay between its covers.

Needless to say, the publication of the unexpurgated *Lady Chatterley's Lover*, and the subsequent court case, aroused great curiosity. As with *Spycatcher* in more recent times, once the book was freely available, the desire to read it evaporated overnight. The fact that D. H. Lawrence's book remained proscribed at Malvern, if not in the world outside, ensured that we all had a go with it under the bedclothes, with rapidly diminishing enthusiasm. And I could not see, for the life of me, why the author should be elevated to that unlikely trinity, with Freud and Stravinsky.

The truth is that I was frustrated and disturbed by compulsory chapel every day, with its emphasis on sin, guilt and unquestioning patriotism. Here was a religion with which I was out of sympathy in harness with a social and political view of the world which I knew in my gut was perverse.

How I wanted to be corrupted, just a little! How I longed for someone who could make sense of it all, who was not frightened by the world of the senses, who I could talk to and who would listen, who would challenge and question. Someone for whom affection, love even, was not associated with secrecy and fear. But in that place, where boys wanted to be thought men, and many men wished they were still boys, Homophobia, that shagged-out Queen, held sway. And disastrously, too many of us, myself included, became for a time her minions.

Sneaking into Worcester to see the double bill of *Love is my Profession* and *Camp on Blood Island* was, like so much forbidden fruit, more exciting in the anticipation than in the tasting. It was certainly no substitute for the talk our greatly respected housemaster thought we needed when most of us had reached our sixteenth birthdays.

'I know self-abuse is quite fun,' he murmured self-consciously. 'But it is a bad habit. Look, I don't know whether I'm telling you about something you know nothing about.'

We had been doing little else for the past three years!

'But you must be warned that masturbation, that is, I believe, the correct medical term for what I am talking about . . .'

The ten of us that had been summoned to his living room, sat like statues, scarcely daring to glance at one another in case we collapsed in hysterics.

'. . . is not a good habit. It saps your energy. You can over do it. You might even get to like it too much . . .'

Harper, known as 'Ding', like his brother before him, on account of his large testicles, started to shake and quiver.

'You see, everybody has done it – '

Daniel hadn't, or so he boasted.

'I mean . . . I admit . . . I . . .'

Oh no! Please don't tell us. Please!

'I've done it myself . . .'

Oh . . . too much! Harper spluttered into his handkerchief, trying to make it sound like a sneeze. We all crossed our legs and shifted around in unison. This once in five years intrusion into the privacy of our embryonic sex lives was as ill-judged and confused as my previous headmaster's baffling homily about 'summoning up the seed'. And why this obsession with masturbation? What else are we supposed to do at a single sex boarding school in which all forms of physical affection are regarded as taboo? And why should sex reduce this otherwise articulate and well regarded man to spluttering incompetence? Of course our reaction to his talk was childish, but in that particular area of our lives, we were still children. And many are the adults I have met since who remain children as far as their own sexual awareness is concerned.

The true 'English disease' is not homosexuality, or a fondness of flagellation. It is sexual immaturity born of single sex boarding schools. Thus, it is rife amongst those whose parents have (or had) the funds to educate their children privately. If child abuse is a serious, topical issue, the isolation of boy from girl, sometimes from as early an age as five until eighteen, should be roundly condemned. And it is just as damaging for young homosexuals to be isolated from members of the other sex as it is for young heterosexuals. (Paradoxically, one of the reasons heterosexual males hate homosexuals is that the latter can have such intense and private relationships with women, of which heterosexuals become bitterly jealous!) To be physically and emotionally retarded by the circumstances in which one is forced to live and grow can only be a bad thing. It was bad for us teenagers, and it was bad for the adults into whose care we were entrusted. Many of them (but, mercifully, not all) were victims of similar abuse from which they had never recovered or escaped. Thus, they passed on to us their inhibitions, their sexual morbidity, their homophobia, their terror of physical rejection.

After five years in which my real self retreated into a black cavern, I left school with six O levels and an A level in History. I failed English Literature! I was unhappy, with little confidence or self-respect. I felt betrayed and humiliated. I didn't like anyone much, not even my own family.

At ten years old, I had been a lively and happy boy, shocked by my father's death, but full of curiosity and energy. Eight years later, I kept anger at bay with music, cinema and books, wondering who I really was and what on earth I was going to do next.

I've just had a phonecall from Michael Darlow to say that he would like to read part two of my film script *Special*. I must set to work at once and prepare a new draft.

A couple of hours later, I've had a call from John Metcalf in Canada about the opera, *Tornrak*. Everything is fine, he says. He is getting on fast with the score and there are plans for Mike Ashman, the proposed director for the WNO production, to do a preliminary production in Banff, Alberta, during March of 1990, with the WNO set which is to be built over there and then flown to Cardiff! John is coming over to Britain at the end of July and is planning to play me the whole score on the piano!

And more good news! Joy Westendarp, my agent, tells me that there's to be a new production of *Rents* in Israel in Hebrew! And a new production of *Lent* in France in French. And *Midnight Feast* is getting an airing at the Edinburgh Fringe Festival this year.

Strange business I'm in. Everything quiet one moment, then buzzing the next.

July

A sparrow, born this year into my garden, has a cancerous growth around its beak and protruding from its right eye. Birds so often appear perfectly created that its disfigurement is shocking on first encounter. But it has great vigour and feeds daily at my window ledge, where I put food each morning. I have studied it with binoculars and am quite sure that the growth is indeed what I think it is, and not part of a chestnut sticky-bud that will drop off in time, which I have also observed in previous years.

When I draw the curtains in the morning, the garden birds set up a tremendous tweeting and gather in the branches of the apple trees. If I over sleep, the bluetits come and peck against my bedroom window to wake me up, so used are they to my habits and the regularity of their breakfast. Mine is the only house here, and I am the only inhabitant. They are still wild, but I fit into their perception of what the world is and who lives in it. When I woke to find a magpie stabbing a small bird to death with its vicious beak, I stalked and eventually shot the magpie. Faced with the choice, I side with the small birds every time.

Once, I was working in my study when that most secretive of birds, a wren, flew into the window pane with a small thump. I went outside to find that it had fallen, unconscious, into an upturned dustbin lid full of water. The wren was drowning. I picked it out carefully and warmed it in my hands, blowing air gently in its face. After some time, its eyes opened and it nestled in a daze in my open palm. Wrens live in little caves, hidden places. Very carefully, I put it in a place of safety and returned to my writing. About five minutes later, there was a fluttering of wings at my window and the wren, against its usual nature, came and sat the other side of the glass, shaking its head and making its distinctive peeping call.

As for the sparrow with cancer, I'll feed it and watch for it, and hope the winter isn't too severe. It doesn't realise it's ill. The other birds treat it normally. Maybe I'm the only one who knows it has tough times ahead.

'Is *Special* supposed to be a farce?'

Michael Darlow, director and producer, and I are sitting at a table on the pavement near the London Post Office Tower. The sun is shining, as it seems to have done for most of the summer, and we are sharing a pot of tea. The previous day, I went to a most enjoyable party that Michael and his wife, Sophie, gave at their home. We had planned to talk about my film script then, but it proved impossible.

'I don't think it's a farce, Michael. It is funny in places, but that's not the same thing.'

'No . . .'

'My purpose is deadly serious. *Special* is partly about the nature of law and order in the country, as opposed to the city. It's not something that is widely understood or written about. It is also about someone ... Kenny ... who feels too conspicuous where he is living and longs for anonymity. Everyone knows a great deal about everyone else in the country. Secrets require great concealment. Even then you're not quite sure what people know, or don't know, about you.'

'Now think carefully about what I'm going to suggest. OK?'

Michael pauses and I note mischief in his eyes.

'Go on ...'

'How about if Kenny was played by a girl? I'm not saying re-write anything.'

'She's still called Kenny?'

'Yes.'

'She dresses like a boy in leathers and rides a motor bike?'

'Yes.'

'And everyone knows she's a girl really, but treats her as though she was a boy?'

'Exactly!'

'That's a really good idea, Michael. It'll be a very odd film. Haunted by the suicide of her father. When Peter pierces her ear with a dart, it'll seem even more like a rape.'

'I know ...'

'Yes ... I'll buy that.'

'Good. And I don't think you've done anything very original with General Hackforth.'

'Right ...'

'You need to think more about him.'

'Right.'

'Otherwise ... I'm really interested.'

'What do we do next?'

'I'll write some letters. Leave it with me. OK?'

Michael looks at me, his eyes twinkling. The hunt is on – *Special* is back in business!

The remaining two British Medical Association videos that I wrote a few months ago are about to be made, back to back. One is about an HIV patient whose immune system is showing signs of breaking down, and the other concerns a doctor who is confronted by his first intravenous drug abuser, who has turned up at his surgery for a free fix. After the near fiasco of the previous video, which was an ambitious re-write of someone else's work, I am cautious about how best to involve myself with the present scripts.

This time, the director is Able Goodman, about whom I know nothing. My scripts are far better worked through as drama, with the confrontational situation of the surgery, and I know that they should work well without causing major problems to anyone.

I decided that I should attend the read-throughs to discuss the scripts with the cast and director and answer any questions, or make any final alterations that might be necessary. I then thought it would be best to stay away from the actual filming.

As before, the casting was extremely good. Actor John Cunningham made a good challenge about finding out about the results of a blood test over the telephone. It was something that both I and various BMA luminaries, and front line medical experts had missed! Otherwise, the scripts were accepted as written, which is as it should be, at that stage of the project.

In the three days following, both scripts were recorded without mishap or unreasonable problems. No bad temper. No confrontations. No bad blood.

Last year I was asked to give a talk in the Purcell Room at the Queen Elizabeth Hall on the South Bank as part of a series concerned with people working in the Arts. I tried to persuade any writers present not to work on word processors. This was intended as a warning of the dangers of using such machines. I had better admit that shortly after giving this Luddite advice I bought an Amstrad PC1512 DDCM (if you want to know precisely) and am working on it now.

The technology of writing has changed since 1974 when I started trying to earn a living solely from what I might once have accurately described as my pen. Quill, nibbed dip pen, fountain pen, biro, pencil, typewriter, word processor ... I started by typing up a fair copy from heavily corrected biro drafts. My typing was slow and littered with mistakes that I described as 'typing errors', as though it was the machine's fault, not mine.

I worked my way through three, cheap, manual machines before buying an electronic, daisy wheel typewriter, with a limited memory, a spell checker and built-in correction tape. The technology was primitive compared to the most basic word processor, but the advantage was that each new draft was typed out from beginning to end to produce a fair copy. This meant that I had to reconsider everything that I had written, every word, every phrase. And that is the important point.

The big danger of the word processor (and it remains a major problem) is that the writer is tempted to leave so much of the first draft in its crude form. Yes, it is easy enough to delete and add text, and to shunt paragraphs around from one part of the draft to another, and so on. But even so, the writer is not compelled by the technology to reconsider everything carefully as in former times.

The reason I was forced into eating my words and buying a personal computer was that working on the two-hour TV script of *Inspector Morse*, with its constant re-writes, was proving too laborious using a typewriter alone. Zenith, the excellent production company, and producer, the late Kenny McBain, assumed that my re-writes would be fed into a word processor, and therefore I could produce a fresh draft of a long script in a couple of days. I did my best on my electronic typewriter, but wore myself out, becoming dizzy with fatigue and making more and more typing errors as a result.

Production companies have come to expect instant copy, instant results. The writer has become an extension of the word processor. Do this, do that, what about if . . . and the writer is expected to press a few buttons and produce the result in the form of a beautifully printed manuscript. Previous drafts, unless meticulously copied from one floppy disc to another, get lost in the process. American universities who have kept many an aged and spent writer in bread by buying up manuscripts, notes, drafts and letters for their archives, will, in the next century have to make do with floppy discs. And because such discs can be endlessly cloned, who is to say which is the true original manuscript of some great (or less than great) masterpieces? The hand-written manuscript is almost extinct. My own handwriting has lost its form and shape. I can sign a credit card bill, or scribble a postcard, but the art of handwriting has not been in such danger since medieval times.

And as I press F2 and then select 'Save' to write the above into 'July. 01', before cooking my lunch, I do so with relief that the process is so easy, but guilt that so much is also in danger of being lost.

Both the First and Second Haltwhistle cricket teams are doing very well in the West Tyne League. Our First Eleven can win the title if they play and win all their remaining matches. I have enjoyed almost every minute of captaining the Second Eleven and have a batting average of 55 at the moment, thanks to some big 'not out' scores.

Hot, dry summers favour the batsmen. The wickets are firmer and truer, and the outfields fast enough to give a good shot its due. If the Second Eleven hadn't lost the services of both its opening bowlers through injury at the start of the season, we would probably be top of the league ourselves.

A great asset has been the rehabilitation of Chris Anson, a young man of immense physical strength and untapped talent, who had dropped out of playing regular cricket. I spoke to him before the season started, saying how much I hoped he would make a comeback this year, and I knew he was keen to do well. Then he jumped into the River Tyne for a Third World charity, landed on a rock and broke his ankle!

Midway through the season, Chris could play with a hobble and found himself being used as a batsman and a bowler (off a few paces) while my two regular openers recovered from their own injuries.

Two examples of his special talent will show what a devastating secret weapon he can be. Against title chasers West Wylam, we got them all out for 105 and found ourselves 4 wickets down for about 10 runs. We looked beaten, but then it started to rain. We agreed to try and complete the match, in spite of the conditions. They were convinced that they had the match sewn up. In came Chris Anson, who hit the wet and slippery ball all over the ground, scoring 48 in 3½ overs. He was caught out on the boundary, leaving our tail enders 20 overs to score 20 runs, which they did to win the match.

Against Haydon Bridge, we got them all out for 78 but found ourselves struggling at 34 for seven wickets down. Chris came in, settled things down, then hit 22 off one over to win that match as well.

The night I returned home from the read-through of the BMA scripts, I got a phonecall from a Newcastle friend who told me that actor Michael Sundin had died that weekend and was being buried the next day. I had heard that Michael's immune system had been breaking down, but was still shocked when I heard that he died, finally, of liver cancer. He was twenty-seven years old.

I met him first in a Newcastle bar in 1975. He was of angelic appearance, with a mop of curly, blond hair. In his short life, Michael was the world trampoline champion, a star of the London production of *Cats*, a *Blue Peter* presenter for BBC TV, in the world touring company for *Starlight Express*, and had many other TV and film credits to his name. He was an entirely good person, without malice, and generous with affection. He loved dancing and was a spectacular tumbler, throwing in combinations of flick-flacks, forward and backward mid-air somersaults, yet always seeming to land on his feet in total control and with an impish grin on his face.

Michael was short-listed for the part of Donald in the film version of *Accounts*, but it was decided, rightly or wrongly, that he was too small for the part. He wanted to do it so badly that it was agony telling him.

'You'll write a play for me one day, won't you?'

'Yes ... yes. I will. You're doing so well anyway, Michael,' I told him. 'When you can't do your acrobatic dancing so easily, then we'll do a play together. Let's keep it in the larder for a rainy day.'

The *Mirror* newspaper ran a deplorable feature about Michael's gayness soon after he had left *Blue Peter*. Sadly, Michael was persuaded to humiliate himself by saying he had never really been gay, and was now heterosexual and how he had been used, and all that trash. Michael (and his agent) should have told the *Mirror* to fuck off.

His funeral service took place at the graveside. It was, of course, profoundly sad. His family stood around the open grave, while his gay friends, of whom I was one, stood discreetly apart. At the end of the Catholic service, a gentleman came around inviting some of those present back to the family house, but, pointedly, not us. It was as though we were, by nature of our collective homosexuality, in some way responsible for Michael's tragic death. I imagine that such tensions have become a regular feature of AIDS related funerals, and I wonder if this is what the play I once promised Michael should be about. His young brother did come round and suggest that we came too. But I decided to slip away quietly, which appeared to be the true wish of the family, even if dear Michael, whom we all loved, would have wished otherwise.

According to myth, the sixties was Woodstock, flower power, liberated and rebellious youth and a re-writing of the rule book. Am I alone in feeling quite apart from all this? I was seventeen years old in 1960, which, if the myth is true, was exactly the age at which the sixties should have made their greatest effect.

But by seventeen I had turned my back, for better or worse on Elvis, Little Richard, Gerry Lee Lewis and the other teen idols of the hour, although I had flirted with them all for a year or two. I was drawn instead to opera at Sadlers Wells and the affordable Gallery Slips at Covent Garden. For me, the 60s meant Birgit Nilsson, Windgasson, Frick, the young Jon Vickers, and the completion of Decca's recording of Wagner's *Ring*. I copied out sections of the *Tristan und Isolde* libretto in German and English from a piano score borrowed from the local library so I could follow what was happening on my second-hand highlights LP. I purchased a VHF radio tuner to listen to BBC music broadcasts in the best possible sound, and made my own 'off the air' recordings, spending hours locked away in my bedroom while most of my contemporaries were out partying. Was I alone? I seemed to be.

Of course there were parties from time to time. For a while, Square Dances were all the rage in Westcliff-on-Sea. With a small band and a caller in the obligatory checked shirt, we pranced around doing Eightsome Reels and not particularly Gay Gordons, whooping in what we presumed was authentic Highland ethnic style.

Then (Oh gloom and despair!) there was the dreaded last waltz, in which all the parents and grannies sat around the perimeter of the floor while their gangly treasures (us) had to pair up for a smoochy, cuddly, goodnight dance. Half the lights in the hall would be switched off to give a hint of intimacy to this ghastly ordeal. Of course, to be left out of this ritual, and be seen to be siding with the grannies rather than the young bloods, was unthinkable. Feeling biochemically unprogrammed for such occasions was no excuse, and I was inevitably dragged on to the floor by the same nymphet who pursued me unmercifully. She had a gap in her front teeth and when she slapped her mouth against mine, would inject great gobbules of saliva as she stuck her repellent tongue into my mouth. At the end of three and a half minutes of this appalling baptism, the music would end, and I would rush into the washroom going 'Urrr! Urrrr! Disgusting!' and spit into the sink, washing my mouth out with water.

'Why am I doing this? Where's the Perseus who will save me from this Gorgon? I could be listening to Mozart. What's the connection between her foul tasting tongue and my cock? I'll never dance again! Never ever! Girls are HOPELESS! Thank God for Benjamin Britten!'

Thank God indeed! The 60s were a marvellous and exciting time in which Britten was producing a regular flow of great music. I heard (and recorded) the first performances of the *War Requiem*, the Cello Symphony, *Curlew River*, and many concerts from the new Maltings, Snape (before the fire). The BBC were always on hand for such occasions. I thought at the time that the Cello Symphony was worth a thousand Woodstocks, and I haven't changed that opinion.

My enthusiasm led me to write, out of the blue, to John Culshaw, then head of Decca's Classical division, telling him how important his work was to me and how much I wanted a job in the record industry. The fact that I couldn't tell a minim from a crotchet did not deter me one bit. To my astonishment, I got a phonecall the following day from the great man himself, asking me to come at once to see him! I couldn't believe it! I got changed and caught the next train to London.

Two hours later, and feeling like the impostor I certainly was, I was shown into John Culshaw's office. He asked me about music and my ignorance must have been obvious, but I did know a great deal about the recorded repertoire and who sung what in which opera set. I knew the Gramophone catalogue off by heart (and still do) and had all sorts of ideas about what Decca should record next. I made out a case for Humperdinck's *Hansel and Gretel* and said what a marvellous opportunity it would provide for a stereo spectacular. I'm surprised he didn't show me the door!

Instead, I was taken off by Jack Boyce, who was in charge of sales (I think), and we had a tea party together in his office. He treated me with a kindly interest that surprised me.

'The trouble is, Michael, that we don't have a job for you right now.'

'Oh...'

'But why don't you get a job in one of the London record stores and learn something about the trade from the inside?'

'Right...'

'How about Harrods? Hang on...'

He picked up the phone and was on to the Harrods Classical

Records buyer before I could open my mouth. Moments later, I had an appointment to see the buyer for an interview.

'Michael, you go off and see him now. You know how to get there? Have you got enough money for the tube fare? Let's see how you get on, and if a job comes up with us, we'll get in touch. OK?'

I worked at Harrods for four months over Christmas. Adding another string to my bow, I also applied to Borough Road teacher training college and was offered a place. I was then sent by Jack Boyce to interview for a job with Argo Records, a Decca subsidiary. Andrew Raeburn and Harley Usill advised me to take the opportunity of being a student for three years. If I wanted to, I could always apply for jobs in the record industry later. Sound advice, gratefully received. The following September, I started training to be a teacher. But I still remember the people at Decca and Argo with great affection.

For most of the time, neither the press nor the public are particularly interested in writers. Very few become household names, or, indeed want to be. When people ask you what you do for a living, they usually greet your answer with the same, stock questions.

'Where do you get your ideas from?'
'Do you have a daily routine?'
'Have you had anything on television?'
'Do you write comedies or serious plays?'

Somehow, you have to be polite and look as though you're answering the questions for the first time. I used to ask why having something on TV was so important, but now I tend to react gently to make life easier. The regular assumption that comedy and seriousness of purpose do not go together says something about the British attitude to drama, and a failing in basic education. I have noticed that Americans tend not to include this dumb question in their litany, suggesting that they treat live theatre with more respect and understanding than the British, who take the opportunity to attend live theatre performances for granted rather than something special and valuable.

The press's interest in writers is generally centred around new plays and it is very much to its credit that a low budget production in some tiny, out of the way venue is often accorded the most careful attention. A new stage play anywhere in London is given far more press coverage than most TV plays. In the theatre, the playwright is still at the centre of attention, while on television the leading actors and occasionally the director hog the publicity. As a result, there is more opportunity for a playwright to make a name for him or her self in the theatre than as a television writer. As far as earning a living is concerned, television is a far safer bet. Few theatre writers who plough steady furrows far from the commercial West End make much more than a most paltry income.

Nevertheless, for a couple of weeks before an opening night, the playwright is likely to be buzzing around town as one of the few dispensible people connected with the new production, to be interviewed by all and sundry. When *Accounts* was produced at the Hudson Guild Theater in New York a few years ago, I was even provided with a press agent whose job it was to arrange four or five interviews a day, including TV chat shows. I did the Nick Yani live, late night show and the venerable Joe Franklin Show. Both in London, and far more so in New York, there is this hungry media animal waiting to gobble up the latest event.

The playwright has to cope with this on an irregular basis, perhaps once every two or three years, and it does require a lot of acquired technique for most of us to survive the course in one piece. Our interviewers, on the other hand, do their jobs from day to day, year in, year out. As a result, they are generally not in the least interested in you or your damned play. You are just another trick. To assume that they are enthusiastic about you or your work, or indeed, know anything about who you are or what previous work you have done, is a grave error.

British journalists are generally less personable than their American counterparts. In London, you can expect moody aggression and no preparation from your harrassed interviewer. A Walkman tape recorder is dumped in front of you and you can expect to be asked, 'What, briefly, is your play about? Oh . . . and what else have you done? Should I have heard of you? Oh! Did you write that? A friend of mine saw it . . . at least, I think they did.' When you read the published article, it contains as much fiction as your new play.

You can also expect a tabloid attitude even from our better newspapers. 'You're homosexual, aren't you? Do you have a lover? How many lovers do you have? Do you have much gay sex?' The *Sun*? The *Mirror*? Wrong! The *Guardian*!

As daunting as anything is the TV chat show. The audience is loyal to the host rather than the guest, and any attempt to score points off your interviewer is ill advised. The reason you are on the show in the first place is to promote your play and sell seats. So, obviously, if you want to play the game by the rules, you don't want to alienate the audience.

On the Joe Franklin Show in New York, I was expecting to be asked about *Accounts* and sheep farming, or rugby football in the Borders. But instead Joe's first question was, 'Britain is now a third rate world power. What's it like to be a great nation in decline?' With more experience, maybe I would have coped better, but my mouth fell open and I spluttered some nonsense about not wishing to return to Victorian values which didn't seem so great to me. A reference to 'the dreadful Thatcher' got a laugh, but Oh! How I wish I'd had my wits about me! The point to remember is that one of the ways chat show hosts approach a guest they know nothing about (I met Joe Franklin for the first time on set, on camera) is to bowl a bouncer at your head to knock you off balance. Next time, I'll be ready.

Only once have I refused to be interviewed by someone (the *Guardian* again!). I had reasons, of course, but on reflection, I over-reacted. Those few days before opening night are very tense, and the playwright is under a lot of pressure. What the British interviewers have to learn from their American counterparts is good natured politeness and professionalism. Too often British journalists have failed to read the press hand out supplied by the theatre, or find out anything about the person they are interviewing in advance. This never happened to me in New York, where I was having my first production and was entirely unknown.

So a playwright's interview checklist might read:

1. Try and look interested and enthusiastic, even if this is the twentieth interview of the week and the interviewer is unprepared and unprofessional.
2. Don't answer questions of a highly personal nature, and if necessary, tell the interviewer to get stuffed.
3. Don't even see anyone from the tabloids. They're shits working for shitty newspapers.
4. If an accompanying photographer asks you to take your shirt off, decline! (Yes, that's happened to me.)
5. Never go to a TV interview in a white shirt. It tends to glare under the lights.
6. Don't try to appear more clever than your TV host, even if you are.
7. Watch out for that lethal bouncer of an opening question on camera.
8. Try to arrive twenty minutes early for every interview. You need time to settle yourself down, take a pee etc.
9. Work hard yourself to get the best out of your interviewer. That's part of your professional responsibility.
10. Carry your own supply of press releases about the play, and your own personal C.V. Interviewers generally claim that they haven't received theirs at the office.

'I was evacuated to Canada. When? 1940. I was fourteen years old. We went up to Liverpool in the train. I knew something special was happening. My father had a big box of chocolates for us, which was really unusual. It was only at the last moment we realised that we were saying goodbye to our parents.'

I was having lunch with my agent, Joy Westendarp, at Solanges off St Martin's Lane. We were sitting at an outside table in the sunshine.

'Which part of Canada?' I asked.

'Nova Scotia!'

'You were with a family there?'

'Not in term time. Only in the holidays. One of the other ships carrying children was sunk by the Germans. *The Benares*. They didn't tell children much in those days. I had this awful feeling about my mother.'

'What was that?'

'Well ... I know this sounds daft ... anyway ... I thought she'd be taken by the Germans and put on a stud farm!'

'A stud farm?'

'You know. An Aryan stud? She was very beautiful, with light red hair. I thought they'd make her have lots of Aryan babies!'

'Were you happy in Nova Scotia?'

'Not very.'

'When did you come back to England?'

'1944.'

'Before the war had ended?'

'Yes.'

'Why?'

'I got sent home early.'

'Why?'

'I was very naughty.'

'What did you do?'

'Men!'

'Men?'

'Men!'

'In 1944 you were ... 16?'

'I know! I used to leave messages for them ... in drain pipes ... under stones ... you know ... that sort of thing.'

'So they thought it was better to risk your life on the Atlantic than have you loose about Nova Scotia?'

'I suppose they did! On the way over, a German submarine stopped the ship in front of us and made the captain hand over all the Italians working on the ship. They were put into a life raft and set adrift. We spent a day or two searching, but never found them. They thought the Italians had let them down. Very cruel. Poor Chef!'

'What happened to you back here?'

'I went to Central Drama School. Then I got offered a job at the Arts Theatre. It was Norman Marshall's company in those days. I worked as an ASM and did bit parts in the evenings. I was with the company that went on tour to Berlin in . . . 1948?'

'To Berlin?'

'Yes.'

'Which plays?'

'*Hamlet* and *Man and Superman*! All of it! It was interminable! The Germans loved it!'

'*Man and Superman* in Berlin in 1948?'

'Yes! What's your duck like?'

August

John Metcalf took me into the recital room at Canada House in Trafalgar Square. He had flown over from Calgary a few days previously and settled himself and his young family in a cottage in Wales for the summer vacation. We always meet in the foyer of the English National Opera, where there's somewhere to sit, a public telephone and someone on duty who will assist with messages if necessary.

'There are a few surprises, Michael,' John tells me as we take the cover off the grand piano.

He sets out the score of *Tornrak*, neatly written in pencil.

'I've re-done the whole of the first scene for a start!'

'Good!'

I'd heard the first scene of Act One and two thirds of Act Two at Banff, Alberta, last December. John had set an edited down version of my opening scene and I had found it too brief and not at all convincing. One of John's many strengths has been his willingness to recompose and re-think parts of the opera, even after he had written out the whole of Act One in full score, which is a most laborious process. In fact, what I'm about to hear is a new version of Act One, and that includes many changes that John has made to my original libretto. I encouraged him from the start to think creatively about the material that I submitted and to edit my text as he thought best. But that did not stop me from saying, 'Look, John! Those lines are important. You really should use them!' when I considered it worth taking a stand about something. This arrangement worked well enough, and the challenge and counter challenge became a regular (and amicable) part of our creative process.

The striking thing about John's Act Two had been that he was thinking dramatically, which was not always the case in his first attempt at the opening Act. John's natural instincts had not seemed primarily directed towards theatrical music. His first attempt at setting my libretto had too much of the concert platform about it. He wasn't seeing the action in his imagination.

Nor was my libretto all that it might have been. Part of my responsibility is to get the best out of the composer and not simply to write my own, private script. Until I'd heard what John's music sounded like and experienced him at work, I could only guess what sort of libretto he might want. Did he like arias, duets, ensembles of various types? Or would he prefer something more Wagnerian? I was to discover that John found setting naturalistic dialogue to music difficult and uninspiring. He much preferred to work in set pieces. He would have been more at home with Lorenzo Da Ponte than Hugo von Hofmannsthal! So I had to imagine a libretto that had already been set to music, with duets, trios, quartets and ensembles of every shape and size. Indeed, my final draft of the opening scene had a section that started as a solo, that became a duet, then a trio, then a quartet, and continued to expand in structure until it involved all the singers, some entering the musical structure as an offstage chorus of sailors. And all this before a note of music had been composed!

I was, I suppose, showing off. And when I heard John's first version, which failed to pick up the gauntlet I had thrown before him, opting instead for his own re-hash of what I had written, I was very disappointed. And I said so. And John, to his great credit, considered the situation and eventually re-composed the entire opening scene.

And that's what I am listening to, for the first time, at Canada House. John plays and sings with great enthusiasm. I've become so used to listening to music that I can translate what I hear into something I understand.

He continues playing and singing, adding a furious nodding to his versatility!

The conditions of the commission allowed us ten or twelve singers and no chorus, so I had to use my theatrical experience to make sure that the artists had time enough off stage to change costumes, or be in the right place for their next entrance, or for singing as an off stage chorus to give the illusion that our resources were far larger than they were.

If John altered the order of things, or edited my work down, as a composer is entitled to do, he was generally motivated by musical, rather than dramatic considerations. My careful control over the movement of our slender resources was occasionally thrown off balance by John's changes to the libretto.

This bothered me more than John, but at the end of the day, it is the composer's opera, not the playwright's. If the director, Mike Ashman, finds he has technical problems with the action, they are likely to be the composer's, rather than the librettist's. It is the composer who finally fashions the structure of the work.

Last December, I prepared lots of re-writes for Act One and left them with John. Now he was through playing the opening scene, I was going to hear what John had made of them. Imagine my surprise when John launched straight into two short scenes that he had added himself, words and music, showing how Arthur was not the sole survivor, and how he had got hold of valuable loot from the shipwreck! In my version, we saw Arthur in a demented state, surviving on his own at an Inuit meat-safe (i.e. dried meat enclosed in a pile of rocks for use by travelling hunters). By adding the extra narrative detail, we do learn a bit more about what had happened to Arthur prior to his dementia, but I'd rather have got deeper into the story more quickly. And precisely how he gained his treasure never really bothered me. The violence that John has added reminds me of Fafner killing Faslot in *Das Rheingold*.

In my version of the story, Arthur Nesbit is a sailor on a trading ship in the 1850s that is heading for the Arctic with a cargo of pots, pans and trinkets to exchange for furs and other goods with the Inuits. Arthur has been behaving strangely and sometimes violently, crying out for Milak to send her 'tornrak', or animal spirit, which, in Milak's case is an Arctic owl. Tornraks (or *tornrait*, to give the word its proper plural) are attached to an individual Inuk for life. Sometimes they are a force for good, and sometimes for mischief. If an Inuk should die violently, his or her tornrak is likely to behave in an enraged and dangerous fashion, although a tornrak's conduct is always unpredictable.

Arthur is taken to the captain and he tells how he has sailed these seas before and is the sole survivor of a mysterious shipwreck that took place some years earlier. How Arthur survived that disaster, what its consequences were, and the true reason for Arthur's presence on board the new ship, all become the dramatic narrative of the opera.

From the outset, I was determined to write a libretto with plenty of narrative drive, so that even an inexperienced opera goer would be swept along by the story. I wanted *Tornrak* to be an opera that everybody wanted to see because it was exciting and moving and spectacular and a tremendous piece of theatre. Although the resources are small by operatic standards (thirteen singers and small orchestra) the piece has the ambitions of an epic.

It is worth remembering that playwrights of my generation are mostly used to writing for casts of six actors or less, because of the economic strangulation to which professional theatre companies have become victim. We are skilled at making a little go a long way. We can only gain experience of writing for larger casts by working with youth theatre groups (like my Haltwhistle Young

Farmers) or other amateur theatre companies. *Tornrak* is the first opportunity I have had, since my career started in 1974, of writing for a professional company whose size has reached double figures!

John plays through the rest of Act One without stopping. I sit behind him, to his right. I cannot read music, or from where I'm sitting, read his small, pencil writing. And there is only one manuscript. I have to listen hard.

As mentioned previously, we had an extended debate about the use of Inuktitut (or the Inuk language) in the libretto. Should Milak sing entirely in Inuktitut in Act One, since that is the only language she knows at this stage? Should she sing entirely in English, so the audience can understand her, although Arthur pretends that she is singing in a language foreign to him? Or should she sing in Inuktitut when addressing Arthur, but in English the rest of the time, so that we are privy to her thoughts?

I had given Milak a substantial aria in which she sings of her dream of being carried off by a great white bird, with many wings, across the ocean, and how she becomes 'a shining captive', soaring high above the world. All this foresees the sailing ship that takes her back to Britain, her fate there, and the climax of the opera, when ... oh ... you'll have to come and see for yourselves!

Anyway, I put it to John that her aria, and much of what followed, would make no sense at all in Inuktitut except to an audience of Inuks. Conversely, John argued that the sounds of Inuktitut and the authenticity of the language were both more important. The confrontation of two different cultures, partly expressed by the inability of the two protagonists to understand each other's words, was a significant part of what I had already written. I said that he was being too literal. Inuks don't go around singing music by Metcalf, with orchestral support. Nobody asks why Aida or her father don't speak a word of Ethiopian, even to each other, or why Madama Butterfly uses nothing but Italian.

The composer (rightly) had the last word. Milak speaks Inuktitut throughout Act One, and the effect, as far as I can judge from what I've heard so far, is interestingly alienating. I might suggest to the Welsh National Opera Company that they print the English translation of *Milak's Dream* in the programme, since there will be no way of communicating the sense of what Milak is singing in production. (Heaven preserve us from distracting surtitles!)

John reaches the end of the Act. He turns to me like a boy who has done something rather naughty, of which he is proud.

'What do you think?'

'I like it.'

'The start is a great improvement, don't you think?' he says, crossing his legs and clutching his top knee.

'Yes . . . much better. It's got a lot of atmosphere. Mysterious. What happened to the screaming tornrak at the end?'

I had concluded Act One with Milak and Arthur being rowed out to a sailing ship, which Milak recognises as 'the great, white bird with many wings' from her dream (all, of course, in Inuktitut now) and with her tornrak, a large, fierce owl, suddenly appearing and screaming at her from the shore.

'Oh . . . do you want that?' says John.

'Yes! It brings the Act to a thrilling conclusion, both visually . . . imagine it, John . . . the boat leaving, the singing in the distance, then, suddenly, this extraordinary bird appearing, and screaming at Milak. She is being severed from her world, which is 'the world' as far as she is concerned, and leaving behind all its spirits and her ancestors, and tornraks and everything. Her owl tornrak sees the danger at once and is screaming at her to return. It really is important!'

'Oh . . .'

'And it sends the audience into the interval surprised and astonished, and wondering what is going to happen next.'

He's not convinced.

'What do you think of the rest of it?'

'I like it. I love the polar bear hunt. I like the spirits of the Inuk hunters. Are they on or off stage?'

'Off.'

'I love the way you have the spirit of the bear throat singing after it has been skinned. That's excellent. The killing of the animal in Act One has a spiritual significance, contrasting with what happens to the brown bear at the fair ground in Act Two.'

'I'm a bit worried . . .' starts John, hesitantly, 'about the lack of lyricism? Is that the right way of putting it? So much happens. So much action . . .'

'Your two new scenes add to the action.'

'Yes, but I wanted them . . .' he says.

'The bear hunt is lyrical . . . and the off-stage songs,' I suggest. 'Look . . . when you've written the final scene of Act Two . . . the duet between Milak and Arthur . . . why not feed back a bit of that into Act One? I assume it will be a big, lyrical number? Maybe, when Milak first enters, you can foreshadow a bit of that final scene. Perhaps some soaring line? The audience will also have the chance to recognise it when it appears again at the end of the opera.'

'Maybe . . .'

'Leave it for now. Get the final scene of Act Two done . . .'

'. . . there are other changes I want to make to Act Two. Not many. The opening fair ground scene. It needs opening up more.'

I nod enthusiastically.

As we put the dust cover back on the piano, I ask John about the arrangements for the preview performances at Banff in February, prior to the official world première in Cardiff in May.

'Richard Armstrong is probably coming over to conduct. Mike Ashman and Bernard Culshaw (director and designer) will be there, of course.'

'But what do you want me to do?'

'I'd like you to be there if possible.'

'At what stage? Wil you be sending me my air ticket as before?'

'Oh . . .'

He hesitates.

'I don't think we've budgeted for that.'

I'm taken aback.

'You've got to fly me over, John.'

'I'll check it out when I get back.'

I cannot believe what I'm hearing. I hope there is some mistake. John thanks me profusely, and sincerely, for all my work on the libretto.

'Well, Michael, your work on *Tornrak* is just about finished.'

Finished? Before rehearsals have even started?

Back in Northumberland, the West Tyne League has only a handful of matches to go, and Haltwhistle First Eleven is still top, with the Second Eleven in second position. With one or two First team players on holiday, Chris Anson and I are drafted into the First team for a crunch match against title chasers Newton. It was a tense, low scoring contest. To my surprise, I ended up with the highest score of the day with 34. We totalled a little over 100, but when it was their turn to bat, they became over cautious, with a low score to chase, and started to lose wickets. We bowled them all out and won the match.

Meanwhile, the depleted Second Eleven lost to Newton Seconds at Haltwhistle, which did our chances of doing the double no good. The benefits of having players like Anson and myself in the Second team are that we get more batting practice each week, so when we move into the First Eleven to cover for missing players, we do so with confidence and with plenty of runs to our credit. Also, the Second Eleven, which contains young players who will become the core of our First team in seasons to come, gets the encouragement and experience of older players who know their way around. They are learning tactics and field placing and the bowlers are gaining in strength and confidence.

As captain, I never get angry with anyone, if something goes wrong. I don't want to undermine a player's confidence. If someone tries his best to take a catch and drops the ball, my method is to pick him up and say 'Well tried! Great effort!' They know that I always expect them to go for everything, which means diving full length in the field, if necessary. If they try their best, I'm satisfied.

As for batting, I have always used seventeen-year-old Graham Lee as one of the openers, often using Chris Smith, our young wicket keeper, to accompany him. Graham has a sound defence, but doesn't score fast. He bats right handed, but is a good left arm bowler. In his case, there is too much left hand when he is batting, which inhibits him from driving through the ball. Consequently, he scores with ones and twos. Nevertheless, he has the great merit of being difficult to shift and I have had the pleasure of many good partnerships with him this season.

I put myself in at three and am continuing to score lots of runs. My average is still over 50. This has meant that we have won many matches without the lower order batsmen getting a chance. That's always the problem with a successful team in 42 over matches. Some captains would change the order around to give more players an opportunity to score runs. But my prime motivation is to win each match as convincingly as possible, which means sticking with my openers. Winning is very important to Haltwhistle, and although our tail-end batsmen would love to show what they can do more often, they are very good natured and pleased that their team is doing well.

In the London offices of *Opera Now* magazine, I meet Gwen Hughes, the new sub-editor. I have written a piece about reissues of Britten operas on compact disc, for which she wants to pay me £100 less than my agreed fee. I have appealed, politely, to Antony Peattie for judgement. Changes are in the air. Mel Cooper is no longer editor. Why, I don't know. Has Melot struck again?

Gwen has just returned from a visit to Nimbus Records, who are about to release a series of historic recordings of great singers from the earliest days of the gramophone. They have adopted a new technique called Natural Ambisonic Transfer, which, it is claimed, will let us hear these fabulous recordings as never before. Gwen is very enthusiastic about what she saw and heard.

I give her my review of a new recording of *Tannhauser*, with Domingo in the lead and Sinopli conducting. I know that some reviewers will complain that the great tenor is recording every darned thing, and, not surprisingly, he sounds like Domingo! It really is extraordinary how ungrateful some people are. Who else should he sound like?

The truth is that I have always longed to hear those amazing Wagner tenor roles sung by a voice that was beautiful in quality, never strained, always with a musical line, never shouted or with runs punctuated with aspirates. And that's what Domingo has given us with his Walther, Lohengrin and now his Tannhauser. It's true that his German is less than perfect, but that's a small price to pay. Anyway, Wagner's tenors are often outsiders who have come from another land, so why shouldn't their German sound foreign?

Gwen agrees to set up an interview with Erik Smith, the retiring Head of Artists and Repertoire at Philips Records. Regular *Opera Now* work, as well as being fun to do, is becoming a useful source of income, and this year has paid for the mortgage on my cottage.

However, her plan to get contributors to send back their CDs to start an opera library at *Opera Now* doesn't go down well with me. Reviewers will lose a tasty perk, and you can be sure that the CDs will soon go missing if they are kept around the office!

During my three years at Borough Road College in the sixties, I got involved with a new organisation that ran residential holidays for schoolchildren at various exciting and remote centres around Britain. It was called Colony Holidays after the French Colonies de Vacances on which the idea was based, and was the brain child of Chris Green, a young teacher at St George's, Harpenden.

I went on a two-week training course to learn about the structure of the holidays, and to acquire a series of skills that included songs, story telling, country dancing, a wide selection of indoor and outdoor games, a dramatised outdoor adventure game (called a 'Wide Game'), handicrafts, and mime.

Against the permissive trends of the time, each holiday was intensely structured. The children were divided into *teams* of about six on arrival and given to the custody of a *monitor* (French influence again, not to be confused with the British *prefect*). The monitor (which was the role for which I was being trained) shared the entire holiday with his or her team, which meant sharing the same sleeping accommodation, eating the same food at the same table, organising activities from morning to bedtime. Since the centres were generally remote boarding schools, seeking to earn a bit of extra cash in the holidays, and Welsh castles, which might have passed as hotels if they hadn't been so decrepit, there was a strong sense of adventure about the whole undertaking. And at that time, opportunities for children to go on holiday on their own were few and far between.

I soon found myself looking after six fourteen-year-old boys, who I'd never met before, for a month at Bryn Bras Castle in North Wales. And we had an absolutely wonderful time! After my experiences at Malvern, and the residual bitterness I felt, my month in Wales was the most perfect antidote. It was possible for young and old to live together in a community, even under cramped and difficult conditions, and to be extraordinarily happy together. We explored our part of Wales, played all sorts of adventure games, made kites, sang songs, held concerts of music and drama in front of blazing log fires in what looked like a *Dracula* film set. Beyond being a most positive communal experience, there was no political or religious subtext to the holiday. There was nothing to sell. No hidden agenda.

And I rediscovered part of myself, which had been blotted out at Malvern. The puppet shows of my early days had been put aside for ten years. But the experience I had gained as a young boy re-emerged as a particular skill in devising and staging short plays with the boys in my team. In the sixties, children were far more inhibited about singing, dancing and acting than they have become since. Initially, I had to devise ways of convincing my young actors to take part at all. So, working off the top of my head, I devised exercises and drama games that the boys could participate in, without feeling over exposed, or fear of making fools of themselves. And being with them twenty-four hours a day made it possible to run the lessons learnt from one activity into another.

Thus, we could sing as we walked in the Welsh mountains, act out one of our plays to astonished and amused patrons of the local café, tell stories during handicraft sessions and use the recording of Sibelius' Second Symphony, which we had all heard for the first time the night before, as the basis for our next play.

As an example of education without the traditional formalities, that month in Wales was sensational and never to be forgotten. It formed the basis of my work as a school teacher for the next ten years. It also sowed the seeds of what was to become my career as a playwright.

My flare for 'mime' (which was shortly to be amended to 'drama' in the Colony Training book) was quickly spotted and soon I found myself assisting Chris Green on Monitor Training Courses. Now, I had to devise ways of encouraging forty or fifty students and teachers to try an activity which most of them found embarrassingly difficult even to attempt. I evolved further exercises, handling the entire complement of the Training Course (including Chris and other available Colony staff) at each session.

My method used little games, devised to break down barriers and inhibitions, often noisy and tactile. Then there were periods when everyone was lying on their backs with their eyes closed, and imagining the story or experience I was describing. I was exploring the powers of the senses: smell, taste, texture, colour, sound, various emotional states of mind.

With so many people involved, there was an element of mass hypnosis about what I was doing and I encountered dangers that, in my innocence, I could not predict. On one occasion, I had forty adults lying comatosed, imagining they were seagulls soaring in the sky above a blue sea, looking down at people swimming, ships sailing, fishermen at work and without a cloud in the heavens. Then, quite unplanned, I told them their wings didn't seem to be working properly and they were falling out of the sky! Absolute pandemonium broke loose! People started crying out and screaming. The sounds of terror filled the room, and those who were not affected at first soon got caught up in the hysteria. I had to get those wings working properly again in a short time! Everyone more or less calmed down and I brought them out of the experience as gently as I could and broke for coffee. Until that moment, I had no idea of the power I had over the group or how easy it was for me to manipulate a mass of people.

Unwittingly, I had strayed into psycho-drama, although what exactly was therapeutic about it, I wasn't sure. And why, you may wonder, was I using such methods to train adults to put on ten-minute dramas with children on holidays? My purpose was to alter perspectives on things familiar, to get people to imagine themselves into experiences which can be used subsequently as the basis for a dramatised performance. I was casting one spell so that others could, in turn, cast other spells on small audiences in some remote country house or castle. I was exposing drama's magic, occult side, which I had first encountered as a young child with my puppets, and was now exploring in my group training sessions with adults and in my many small, intimate, and, at best, potent productions with my young actors.

None of my plays was written out. They were all improvised with dialogue or a sole narrator (often myself), and with music either performed or sung by the cast, or off records.

My work with Colony Holidays continued into the early seventies, although I found myself in the role of director (i.e. running the centre) rather than monitor in charge of a specific team of youngsters. This work took me all over Britain. I ran centres on the Isle of Man, up by Loch Rannoch in Scotland, and at Feathersone Castle, near my present house, and at half a dozen other places around the country.

In its earliest days, Colony Holidays was genuinely pioneering in breaking away from traditional educational attitudes and broadening the range of activities that a single teacher might use in his or her profession. Hundreds of teachers trained and worked for Colonies and their newly gained skills and experience were fed back, in turn, to their own professional work in term time.

The Colony organisation flourished and expanded, was mentioned approvingly in the House of Commons (to my surprise) and was the subject of much positive publicity. Specialist Colonies were organised, including a successful association with Puffin

Books. A beautiful house, Linden Manor, situated (ironically for me) on the western slopes of the Malvern Hills, became its administrative headquarters and a holiday centre.

Then things seemed to go wrong. Personally, I was going through my sexual identity crisis. My life was dedicated to teaching, and music and books. I was restless within my celibate's cloak. Chris Green had been on some sort of Encounter group and had been sufficiently chastened by the experience to want to inflict more of the same on to his loyal monitors and directors. I thought that sitting around, telling your best friends what sort of shits they really were did little to promote harmony and happiness. I knew enough about my own sexual and emotional fragility, and that of those around me, not to get involved. I was, and am still, a deadly dangerous person in an Encounter situation. I know far more about people than they ever tell me. Then, I had the power to destroy relationships and marriages, and reduce people to sobbing wrecks. Tearing people apart is not difficult. Putting them back together again is.

I wanted nothing to do with it and quit.

What do I dare tell you about Freddie? Not his real name, for sure! Now, in his late twenties, he's a student in London and shows signs of making something of himself. No. That's unfair. Fred has always been someone special.

I first met him while working at the Traverse Theatre in Edinburgh, Fred's home town. He was mad on theatre and, in another age, would have made a sensational Bluebell Girl. He told me lots of outrageous stories about himself (they all do!), farcical bedroom encounters and midnight escapes that had me 'rocking with laughter', as the billboards outside his private, real-life theatre might have said.

He was, and doubtless remains, extraordinarily naughty. On a crowded 125 express from London to Edinburgh, he once seduced an Australian tourist sitting opposite him with his foot! Slipping off his shoe and sock, he managed to unzip the unsuspecting man's fly with his toes and proceeded to wank him off with his toes! All this in broad daylight in a crowded carriage.

'Michael! I kept getting cramp in my toes and my leg would shoot forward and kick him in the balls! He'd wince but didn't want to give the game away to the woman sitting next to me!'

Then Freddie decided to spend the summer in Greece, living off his wits and playing whatever games came to hand. He used to write me long and detailed letters most weeks. I always wrote back, using the address of the model agency with whom he'd signed up, and slipping in the occasional £5 to help him on his way. His letters were beautifully written and often very funny. An extra long and funny one would get a surprise £10 by return. For Freddie is firmly established as part of my extended family.

In the six months of his stay in Greece, he bummed his way around the islands, sometimes penniless and living on beaches, sometimes playing toy-boy on a millionaire's yacht. He was fast food, easily picked up and discarded. He'd be washing dishes on Mykonos one week and be a cabaret star on Crete the next! His model agency even landed him the prime job of advertising Wrangler Jeans on all the billboards in Greece and then pocketed most of the cash themselves! By the time Fred came back to Britain, he had become the icon of the hour, displayed along the highways, plastered onto the sides of derelict buildings, and adorning many a bedroom wall.

He came home tanned and broke, of course, and got a job in a house of ill repute in West London that described itself as a 'Health Clinic'. There, Fred and the other boys would wait for their wealthy clients and fleece them for every penny they could as safely as possible. Fred's favourite oddity was 'the nipple man', who arrived with carefully washed and ironed white gloves for Freddie to wear. After an established ritual, Fred would don the white gloves and squeeze the gentleman's nipples until he reached an orgasm.

'He was always very polite. When I'd finished squeezing him half to death, he liked me to fold the gloves neatly and pack them away in his brief case. He used to pay quite well. I think he was a judge. That's what the others said, at least. He got dumped on me because the others couldn't do it without laughing, and that humiliated him. I know he was weird, but I rather liked the nipple man.'

I visited Fred at his brother's house, where he is now living while doing Media Studies as a full time student. There used to be a large alsation in the house as well, but the sensible animal decided that it had had enough and it boarded the bus for Victoria Station on its own and hasn't been seen since.

I bought a couple of bottles of wine, which we drank with a few of Fred's friends who were there.

A week later I had a distressed Freddie on the phone.

'Michael, you remember those two boys you met last week?'
'Yes.'
'We were all going out to this party. I arrived late, as usual, and missed the boat. Michael, it was *The Marchioness* . . .'

Some days previously, *The Marchioness* had been struck by another ship on the Thames and sank with the loss of more than sixty lives.

'They were both drowned. I've just had to view one of the bodies. I should have been with them.'

September

After being on the receiving end of numerous interviews connected with my own work, I find myself doing the interviewing for *Opera Now* magazine. My first subject is to be Erik Smith, the retiring Head of Artists and Repertoire at Philips Classical Division. Although I have never met him before, I have known about his work and bought many of his recordings during the past thirty years. I have the highest regard for his achievements as a pioneer in developing the dramatic potential of stereophonic opera recordings during his early days with Decca. His first opera recording as producer was the legendary *Peter Grimes* with Pears in the title role and Britten conducting. His time with Philips is equally distinguished, with classic opera recordings of Haydn, Berlioz, Mozart and early Verdi.

But having been so frustrated at the liberties taken by people who have interviewed me, I wanted to devise a technique that would treat my subject fairly. I thought of using my Sony Walkman Pro, plonking it down on the table and pressing the record button, but decided against this. I would have to edit anything that was said anyway, and that would immediately set direct speech into a fictitious context. Also, a literal transcription of everything that was said would have to include all the pauses, hesitations and grammatical errors. Once a transcriber starts to tidy up the actual words spoken (as happens with transcriptions of debates in the House of Commons that are published in Hansard), then the result also becomes a fiction.

So I decided not to record an interview, and not even to take many notes. I prepared myself thoroughly by reading again about Erik Smith's early days with Decca in John Culshaw's books *Putting the Record Straight* and *Ring Resounding* and made many biographical notes, including lists of recordings that he had produced for both Decca and Philips.

We met in Erik Smith's South Bank apartment. Almost as soon as I had sat down he said, 'What do you think of Harnoncourt?'

Presumably, this was to see whether I knew anything.

'Brilliant one moment, batty the next!' I replied.

'Ummm . . .' said Erik.

'But he does have a genuine and original musical personality,' I added.

'Yes. I think so,' Erik agreed.

To talk to such a man about my favourite subject was a treat for me, and towards the end of the interview I began to wonder how on earth I was going to condense so much fascinating material into an article that was the right length for the magazine. Also, Erik had confided a number of things that he would not want published about some of the artists with whom he had worked. I suppose that if I had been a professional journalist, such revelations would be precisely the sort of things that I would have featured in my article.

I decided to write a draft of the interview from memory and

then submit it to Erik Smith to challenge any of the factual detail, so that I didn't misrepresent anything he might have said. He kindly agreed to this and my article was written, sent to him, had a few points of factual detail amended and then dispatched to Gwen Hughes of *Opera Now*.

Imagine my dismay when I received galleys showing how my article had been re-drafted at her end into a simple dialogue format, as though the piece was a transcript of a recorded interview! Nothing could have been less like recorded dialogue! After spending the past fifteen years of my life writing exclusively for theatre and television, poor Gwen hadn't even bothered to pick up the phone and ask me to re-write the piece myself! There was no personality, no sense of occasion, nothing left of Erik's quiet professionalism as he made instant and important decisions over the phone during my time with him, no drama. Only unconvincing wodges of text, pretending to be dialogue. I did, of course, protest but was told that I wasn't a professional journalist. If that means that I have an unwelcome desire to treat my subject in the fairest possible manner, then I happily accept the charge.

My mother is sitting on bare, wooden boards, on the floor of a terraced cottage in Williton, Somerset. It is early evening and she is speaking to me on the phone with her six o'clock whisky by her side.

'The workmen have been here most of the day. They're very nice. I'm glad they've gone. A bit of peace.'

For some years, she has been talking of buying her own house to live in. Since she married my father before the War, she has lived at Alleyn Court School, besieged in term time by hoards of boys. Now past seventy, she has decided to uproot herself and make a fresh start. She has chosen Williton, which could scarcely be further away from where I live in Northumberland.

'Are you happy there, Mum?'

'Yes.'

'You've got an escape route. You can go back to Alleyn Court whenever you want.'

'Oh yes! It's easy. I just hop on a train.'
'Does it feel strange to wake up in a new house?'
'A couple of times I've wondered where I am and what I've done!'

We talk about unblocking fireplaces, what appears to be growing in the small garden and her new neighbours who have made her feel so welcome. She longs for me to travel down to visit her, which I must do sometime. But taking a week off isn't as easy as it sounds, even for someone who is self-employed. For one thing, the cricket season is coming to an exciting climax for Haltwhistle . . .

Borough Road Training College is near Hounslow in West London. Every few minutes, Jumbo jets come into land at London Airport, just down the road. Conversation becomes impossible, and windows and buildings shake as the monsters approach the runways. I was a student there in the early sixties and found it pleasant and undemanding. I was lazy and content to get by.

For my first year, Borough Road was a single sex institution. Although most students welcomed the advent of women, there was a vocal minority who didn't. They invoked, rather snobbily, that worn out old pimp Tradition, although the true reason had more to do with the homoerotic undercurrent of the place. Looking back, I am far more aware now of its gay sub-culture, both amongst students and staff (especially the recently engaged women lecturers) than I was then. In the manner of the times, I simply could not see, in true focus, what was happening right under my nose.

So I happily got on with my accustomed solitary life, playing tennis and badminton, slipping into the West End to see plays and operas, and drifting along with whatever work had to be done, which wasn't much. The standard of lecturing ranged from solid competence to blithering inadequacy. And the latter gave us all a marvellous excuse to behave in class with a disruptiveness that would have put a gang of rabid delinquents to shame.

Poor Mrs Bee! (I cannot bring myself to disclose her real

name.) Her lectures were a riot, as we reverted to five-year-olds in a state of hysteria. Every time she turned her back to write on the blackboard, forty paper darts would take to the air in a crazy dog-fight. She would finish her chalking and carry on with her nonsense, completely ignoring the devastation that surrounded her. This encouraged us even more, of course. She turned again to the blackboard. Squadrons of darts clouded the skies. Mrs Bee wore her hair in a piled heap that added a foot to her height. Fate decreed that two paper darts should impale themselves in this monument to vanity and stay steadfastly stuck. But nothing could daunt Mrs Bee. She turned round and continued, as though nothing had happened, the two darts sticking out each side of her head above her ears. We gave her a standing ovation, and to this day, I doubt if she knows why.

After a couple of terms of this, we tired of our naughtiness and longed for an excuse to skip her tedious company. But we needed to get ticked in her register to complete the course. So after about ten minutes, I would, with insulting politeness, preface a question with the words, 'Mrs Bee, by way of a conclusion, could I ask . . . ?' As soon as she had completed her first sentence, we would all grab our books and flee the classroom.

Teaching Practice was another matter altogether. My first took me for a few weeks to a ghastly Secondary Modern School, full of grim-faced and sulky pupils who had been bludgeoned into submission by a tyrannical staff. I found myself in the middle of a B feature Horror Movie and longed to dump my Teaching Notes in the nearest bin and walk out of the gates.

When my tutor came to see how I was getting on, the fourth year pupils, whom I had never met before, just sat like Zombies and refused to cooperate in any way. I would ask a question. Total silence. I tried to get someone to read a passage from a book. Total silence. They just sat there, expressionless. My tutor was twinkling away at the back, wondering what on earth I was going to do next. I'd like to report that, as a result of inspirational wizardry, I managed to transform the pupils into active, free-thinking individualists. But I didn't. Departing from my lesson notes, which were, in any case, on my tutor's knee, I introduced and read a few poems, told a story and sang a couple of songs, which did arouse minor surprise.

My tutor was dismayed.

'You should have banged a few heads together! You just caved in. If you ask them to do something, make them do it!'

'That's precisely why they've become the way they are! I can't undo ten years of abuse in these bloody schools in a few minutes. That was my first time with them,' I protested.

'You've got to win the first battle,' said my tutor, who, to give him credit, was one of the better lecturers at college.

'I don't agree,' I replied, stubbornly. 'Teaching isn't a war. That wasn't a battle. Given time, I could do something worthwhile with them.'

'How?'

'Get to know them as people ... as individuals. Play football with them, take trips to the cinema and theatre, give them time to decide for themselves whether I have anything to offer. If they make it clear I don't, I'll quit teaching.'

That was the first clash of many that dogged my teaching career. I never saw my role as purely classroom based. I always wanted my students to think their own thoughts, not mine. I wanted them to question the structures and attitudes of the world about them. I wanted them to challenge authority to discover its true worth. I wanted them to learn to speak out fiercely on their own behalf.

Needless to say, that agenda seldom went down well with my colleagues. I can understand that if you are a chemistry teacher with a fixed and factual syllabus, then classroom activity is clearly defined. But as an English teacher, my brief may indeed be to teach my pupils to read, write, talk and listen. But what are we to read and write about? What should we discuss? Teenagers are interested in sex, money, music, sport, food, adventure, and a hundred and one other things. In the view of other teachers, some of these interests were either too personal or controversial (money, sex, politics) to be written or read about, or discussed freely in

English, while others (music, sport, hobbies) were deemed too trivial for serious, classroom time!

I always argued that what I was trying to achieve would make better chemists, physicists and historians and that my work was an adjunct to that of the other staff. Education is not simply an imparting of a host of facts, coupled with a few basic skills. Education is more properly concerned with helping pupils to make the best use of their acquired knowledge and skills. And if knowledge really is useful, pupils will want to learn more.

That my view should have been seen as subversive, anarchic and anti-authoritarian was preposterous. But, sadly, that was the case, and in the end I did indeed decide to quit teaching. I was worn out, fed up with the institutional intrigues of school life and unable to handle the dirty tricks department of West Denton High School, Newcastle upon Tyne, where I ended my teaching career as Head of the English Department in 1974.

I'm feeling very guilty about not starting to write the play for Elizabeth Quinn. I've been working constantly, without a holiday for some years now, but I never seem to get ahead of what I'd planned to do. The *Opera Now* articles take up a few days, then there are books to read, books to review, about thirty letters a week to write, play scripts (often unsolicited) arriving in bundles most weeks. I could easily spend my working hours as my own secretary, without ever getting down to writing anything original.

At the back of my mind all year has been the saga of *Kameraden*. This is the film that I wrote for BBC TV some years ago about German prisoners at the conclusion of the Second World War. It was put on ice, then Chris Parr (BBC Pebble Mill) took an interest in it again. I started to work on five two-hour films, following the lives of a group of men who first met as POWs in Britain. I had completed detailed outlines for the first six hours (the first two hours of which are in full script) only to be woken up after midnight by Chris to be told that my story was 'too political'. I told him that I didn't see how the story of prisoners being repatriated, and the difficulties of rebuilding lives in a defeated and divided Germany, could be anything other than political. I sent him the next outline, but have never had any acknowledgement or reaction of any kind for nearly a year now.

It is profoundly depressing to feel that all the reading, research and planning that I have done for *Kameraden* has been dumped in some obscure corner at the BBC. I wish I had kept the project to myself and worked on it in my own way and in my own time. I feel tricked into doing the work, only to find myself abandoned. Why no acknowledgement of the receipt of my work? Why no encouragement? Why am I dragged out of bed in the early hours of the morning to be told my work is 'too political'?

I suppose the way to extricate myself is to rush through the two remaining outlines, send them to Chris Parr, get the whole thing rejected, then try and sell it to an independent company that is really interested.

I'm working hard and long hours, and getting nowhere! Michael Darlow will be doing his best to get *Special* off the ground, but Channel Four isn't interested. I haven't heard a word from John Metcalf in Banff about whether The Banff Centre intends to fly me out in February for the two performances of *Tornrak*. I suspect they won't and feel bitterly angry.

Balls to everyone! I'm going to the Sauna!

The cricket season came to a triumphant climax for the Haltwhistle First Eleven, who beat Wylam in a thrilling match to win the West Tyne League title. Batting first, Haltwhistle scored over 200 runs in their 42 overs, which in most circumstances, would have ensured an easy victory. But Wylam fought back like heroes and, in near darkness, needed 4 runs to win off the last ball. Some of the boundaries are short at Wylam, and the outfield is very bumpy, making fielding difficult in bright daylight, let alone after dusk!

Haltwhistle's veteran fast bowler, Vince Collier, was bowling the last over. Vince's run up consists of thirty yards of pounding raw meat, followed by a mighty leap, a snarl, and a whirl of mighty arms. Faint-hearted batsmen have been known to shelter behind the square leg umpire at the sight. With sweat pouring from his creased brow, and every Haltwhistle fielder tense with nerves, Collier made sure the ball was dry and free of mud. Behind the stumps, Brian Hargraves thumped his wicket-keeping gloves together and squatted down expectantly, his short fuse glowing in the gloom. Somewhere out there in the darkness, he knew that Collier has started his run up from the rhythmic quake of the ground beneath his feet. The ball thumped down on a length, the brave batsman threw his bat where he thought the ball might be. He missed! The ball flew through to Hargraves and stuck in his gloves, preventing a certain 4 byes! The batsmen were bound to run anyway, and Hargraves nipped forward to whip off the bails. Triumphant Haltwhistle cries informed the spectators what had happened, and sporting Wylam conceded victory after an epic contest!

October

In 1973, the year before I left teaching to start a career as a playwright, a dramatic incident occurred that was to change the course of my life.

One afternoon, a group of boys came and said that one of their mates was in trouble and needed help. Unknown to me, a pupil I'll call Ben, who was in his final year at school, was living rough somewhere in West Newcastle. For some reason, he was unwilling to return home. They told me that he was developing a bad cough as a result of the cold, damp nights. He needed a bath, some hot food, and a chance to sort things out. Ben had been in my class the previous year, and I had got to know him in school and on the frequent trips to the theatre that I organised in the evenings.

I went at once to Ben's housemaster, the late Brian Richell, and told him what had happened. What should I do? Brian asked me to come back at afternoon break, by which time he would have found out more about the situation.

An hour later, Brian told me that Ben had indeed been reported missing from home. He wasn't wanted by the police, who weren't especially concerned. He was old enough to look after himself. Anyway, he had slept rough before. Brian asked me to send a message to Ben, via the boys who had come to see me, to say that I would take him to my home in the country after school (which was a few miles from Brian's house in Hexham) if that was what he wanted. There, I should let him have a hot bath, cook him a meal, and then take him round to talk to Brian and his wife.

And the end of that Friday afternoon, I went to my car, and sure enough, Ben darted out of nowhere and hopped in, crouching down out of sight. He didn't smell too good and didn't say much. I put the car heater on full because he was chilled through.

When we got home to my place, he had a long, hot bath, while I washed his filthy clothes and cooked for him. He was very relieved to be indoors and have someone to look after him. I asked him why he was refusing to return home, but he wouldn't tell me. (I never found out.) I asked him if he would like to phone his father, but he was startled at the suggestion and refused.

Later, I took him round to Brian's house, where Heather, his wife, gave us coffee and sandwiches. Ben was absolutely determined not to return to his own home. If we tried to take him back, he said he would run away again. I was asked if I would look after Ben during Saturday while Brian tried to find some sort of solution.

As fate would have it, when Ben and I arrived back at my cottage, I was struck down with the worst food poisoning of my life! I found myself being repeatedly sick and feeling like death. Suddenly, roles were reversed and Ben was looking after me. While I heaved and groaned upstairs, Ben did the dishes, attended to the fire, Hoovered the living room and kept poking his head round my bedroom door with hot cups of coffee that he insisted would do me good!

He nursed me through the following day, which was a blessing. While I sat beside the fire, green faced with a bowl at my feet, Ben got busy and painted the stairs and hallway! Then he said he would write me a story. He sat at the kitchen table and wrote furiously for a couple of hours, then waving his story triumphantly in the air announced that he was ready to read it to me. It was an adventure about a boy running away to North Shields to work on a fishing boat.

The following day, Ben's parents, who had been contacted by Brian, arrived unexpectedly. Ben ran out through the back door and hid in my coal shed. It was with some difficulty that I persuaded him to return home with them.

End of story? Unfortunately not.

At the end of school the following Tuesday, I was met by two police officers and asked to drive to a nearby police station. There, I was grilled by the pair of them for an hour and asked if I had buggered Ben! Certainly not! I was then told that Ben had been stripped in the police station, in front of his father, and a doctor had examined his anus. The doctor could not say whether Ben had been buggered or not. Ben had angrily and persistently denied that any such thing had occurred, the police assured me. Why, I asked, had they committed such a dreadful act, in that case? I never received a satisfactory answer to that question. They would continue to investigate me, I was told. I would hear from them again in a few days. I left the police station in a state of shock, and drove back to my cottage profoundly depressed and sickened.

After sitting alone in the dark for an hour, I phoned up Brian to talk to him. He was as stunned as I was, although he had been told what had happened. I went round to his house for the rest of the evening.

Each day, I went to school and taught my classes in spite of the strain of it all and my stomach, which had still not returned to its normal self after the poisoning. Each day ended and there was no news. I went to the headmaster to ask if he had heard anything from the police. He said he hadn't and didn't want to discuss the matter.

The end of the week came, and still I hadn't heard anything. Nor had Ben come back to school. I had no idea what had happened to him. Brian, whose job as housemaster was, I guess, at risk, had been instructed not to discuss the case with me, which isolated me further.

Mrs Clark of Featherstone Castle had heard what had happened and insisted that I spend the weekend there, which was kind and gracious of her. I was feeling dangerously paranoid and needed company and support.

It was not until the following week that the headmaster told me that no further action would be taken. I asked when the police had informed him of this and was astonished to hear that he had been told the previous Friday! When I asked why he had waited till Tuesday afternoon to pass on this vital news, he said he had been too busy!

I also saw the investigating officer again. He was conciliatory and assured me that he was only doing his duty. He claimed that the school, by which I assume he meant either the headmaster or one of his deputies, had asked him to investigate the matter, even though no complaint had been made by Ben or his parents. The fact that I had agreed to help Ben at the request of his housemaster seemed to be consistently ignored by everyone.

Then, to my further astonishment, the officer told me that he had left school early and hadn't sat any examinations. He thought that if he was able to pass a few O levels, it might aid his promotion prospects! Could I help? After what I had been through, I didn't much feel like taking on another student, but gave him instead all the information he needed to attend evening classes. Whether he got his promotion, I have no idea.

As for Ben, after his sexual humiliation at the hands of the police, and contrary to his true character, he snatched a lady's handbag in the street, was caught and detained at a reform school.

Appalled at what had happened to both Ben and myself, I handed in my letter of resignation, to take effect from 1 May the following year. I also resolved that as soon as my teaching career was at an end, I would pull my blurred and celibate sexuality into sharper focus, seeking all the counselling and support that I could find. Among my first plays was *Standard Procedure*, which was based loosely and fictitiously on my experience with Ben. It was published by Iron Press and, in an expurgated form, was produced by BBC Radio's Afternoon Theatre.

More than sixteen years later, I remain stunned by these events. Ben was legally old enough to marry. Old enough to roar around the roads on a motor bike! Old enough to sign up with the armed forces. Young men not much older than him are in uniform, carrying lethal weapons in Northern Ireland. Yet the police were able to humiliate him physically in front of his father and claim that they were doing their duty!

And yes, I was extraordinarily naive to compromise myself by getting involved the way I did. Ben must be in his early thirties now. If he ever reads this, I believe he'll remember how I tried to help when he was in a tough spot, while I shall always be grateful to him for painting the stairs, doing the dishes, nursing me when I was so sick, and for writing me such a good story.

Suddenly it's autumn! The phone hasn't stopped ringing. Why is it that I can go for days without a call, then everybody tries to contact me at once?

Chris Parr of BBC TV Pebble Mill has renewed his interest in *Kameraden*, the film series about what happened to German POWs after the end of the Second World War. He wants the remaining four hours of scenario by Christmas, if possible. Apparently the first six hours are not too political after all!

Actor Richard O'Callaghan phoned and I had to confess that I hadn't written a word of the play that I had in mind for him and Elizabeth Quinn. As it turns out, this isn't the end of the world since Elizabeth is indeed going to play Hedda Gabler in London early in 1990. This is thrilling news and I'm determined to be in the first night audience.

Then, at half past six in the morning, I got a call from an Australian gentleman in Melbourne who had seen the recent Australian broadcast of *Lent*. He told me how much he had enjoyed it, and added that his daughter, who was terminally ill, had been so concerned about the fate of young Paul that she had written to the actor, Graham McGrath, to ask if he was all right.

Very decently, Graham, who is now in his late teens, had written back and sent her his photograph. This had delighted the girl and was one of her prize possessions. How impossible it is, when you write a play, or make a film, to have any idea how your work might affect other people's lives, even years after the event.

My caller's name was Dean Vaughan, who was nothing to do with theatre or TV, he assured me. He was, he said, involved in heavy engineering. However, he was anxious to assist in the funding of my next film! So I told him about *Special* and how director Michael Darlow was trying to raise money to make the film at this very moment. Mr Vaughan promised to help if he possibly could. Whether anything further will come of this generous offer remains to be seen, but naturally I wrote to Michael at once to tell him what had happened, and we will do everything we can at our end to explore the Australian connection. I also wrote to Graham McGrath to thank him for responding to the young girl's letter. Tragically, she died a few weeks ago.

Another phonecall, this time from Joy Westendarp asking if I'd be interested in a new series being written by John Bowen for Euston Films. Producer Steven Gilbert wanted to make contact. I phoned Steven and he told me that *Shrinks* was about a group practice of psychiatrists. It sounded interesting and he promised to post off the first four hours of the script. We arranged to meet in London in a couple of days.

I read the scripts, did piles of notes, leapt on a train and was on the doorstep of Euston Films exactly on time. But John Bowen and Steven Gilbert made it clear as soon as we sat down that they were not interested in what I thought of the first four scripts! All they wanted from me was further storylines to fit into what was there. That might have been OK if I hadn't felt that there were serious weaknesses in what I had read. I was sure that a week or two of re-writing would make the series so much better, but they wouldn't even discuss anything in those scripts. Since I had already done hours of work on them, I wasn't very pleased about this. They tried to get me to discuss my own ideas for storylines, which I thought was premature since there were so many questions I wanted to ask about the series, but was expressly told that I couldn't ask them!

Politely, I wished Steven Gilbert and John Bowen good luck with *Shrinks* and left. What a relief to be back out on the streets!

That night I went to the ENO production of Janacek's opera *Kata Kabanova* and found myself sitting next to Sarah Playfair, administrator of the Glyndebourne Touring Company. She asked about *Tornrak* and we ate ice creams in the interval. And enjoying every moment of that wonderful opera, a psychological study of human behaviour and neurosis par excellence, made me realise what a close shave I'd had with *Shrinks* a few hours earlier. I phoned Steven Gilbert from the Opera House and told him how sorry I was that things hadn't worked out between us and wishing him better luck with another writer.

News at last from Canada! John Metcalf phoned from Banff with news of *Tornrak*. Yes, of course The Banff Centre would fly me out in February. He was most concerned that there should have been any misunderstanding about this. He had completed all but the last hundred bars of Act 2 in piano score. As soon as this was completed, he would set about orchestrating the whole thing. It occurred to me that since rehearsals were due to start in January, there was no time to be lost. John told me also that he had written an extra short scene for the opening of Act 2! In my version, the Act had started at a fairground in Wales, where Milak was being exhibited in a side show as 'The Wild Woman of the Frozen North'. This, I thought, would get the second half of the opera off excitingly, and contrast with the bleakness of the arctic scenes of Act 1. I asked John why he wanted to add another scene. He said that director Mike Ashman thought it was a good idea. I have never met or talked with Mike Ashman, and wondered why no one had asked me what I thought about this! Ashman is about to open a new production of *Medea* at Covent Garden, so I imagine he's got his hands full just now.

In Newcastle, the C. P. Taylor Festival is about to open. I sat in on a morning's rehearsal of *Good* at The Playhouse. Actor David Roper looked interesting as Halder, and Joan Heal, who became a big West End star many years ago with *Grab me a Gondola*, was striking as Halder's mother.

I'll be preparing some rehearsed readings of extracts from C. P. Taylor's plays *Lies about Vietnam*, *Schippel* and *Bread and Butter*. I'm delighted to hear from Live Theatre's Max Roberts that Roy Marsden and Roger Kemp are coming up from London to take part, which is a tremendous boost for all of us.

Max has also shown an interest in commissioning a play from me for production next March. He is planning a season of new plays for production in the Cecil Taylor Studio at Live Theatre's complex on the Newcastle Quayside. This is the first time Live Theatre have made a serious approach to me for more than ten years and I'd like very much to come up with something. I've thanked Max very much for the interest he is showing in me and that I'll get back in touch when I've had time to think about it.

Down to London again, this time for a meeting at the British Medical Association with Dr John Dawson and Norman Burrows, who produced the three BMA videos for the *Foundation for AIDS* that I wrote during the summer.

I'm pleased to hear that videos two and three have been greatly liked by everyone. John Dawson wants to know if I'm interested in scripting another video, this time about the problems that doctors in hospitals face when they have to tell someone that a loved one has died. I agree to help in any way I can.

Secondly, the possibility of a feature length film drama, made under the auspices of the BMA is discussed. The subject is set in the near future and concerns the particular problems of how politicians and others cope with a worsening AIDS crisis. Sad to say, it is John Dawson's firm opinion that the 1990s is going to be a critical decade as far as AIDS and Civil Rights in Britain are concerned.

We discuss possible scenarios. I suggest that we set the film around the weeks leading up to 1 January 2000 and agree to go off and make a preliminary draft about what the scenario might contain. Previously, a leading director was lobbied and expressed an interest in such a project. The plan is for John Dawson to add a page or two, giving his professional opinion on what might happen with AIDS in the next ten years, to whatever I come up with, and then send the whole lot on to our director to see if he is able to help in any way.

'A producer's responsibility can be daunting. You hear a young singer with a sensational voice in the making. If you contract such a talent to record a major role, a career can develop too fast for its own good. A classic example was Elena Suliotis.'

It's the morning of the *Gramophone* Awards, and I have met Erik Smith, retiring Head of Artists and Repertoire of Philips Classical Division, for a second interview.

'Suliotis was only twenty-one or so. Her audition was electrifying and I got her engaged to record Abigaille for Decca the following year, opposite Gobbi's Nabucco. She used her voice most excitingly, but recklessly too. I remember Erich Leinsdorf stopping by at one of the recording sessions. He told Suliotis, in a fatherly sort of way, that if she carried on singing like that she wouldn't have any voice left. She wouldn't listen, but he was right.

'If I hadn't cast her in the role in the first place, would her career have developed at a more healthy pace? Would Elena Suliotis still be one of the great stars of today?'

Erik Smith was silent. He wanted a reply.

I said, 'She would have sung like that whether you had given her a contract or not. At least your recording of *Nabucco* caught her at the peak of her short career.'

'Yes, but without that recording, maybe the great opera houses of the world would not have been falling over themselves to engage her at all costs. Her career, and her voice, might then have developed at a healthier rate.'

'Didn't the first recordings of Suliotis and Montserrat Caballe come out in the same month?'

'I think it was about the same time.'

'I remember hearing their voices compared on Radio Three's *Record Review*. If I'd been forced to put money on which would have the greatest career, I'd have gone for Suliotis.'

Erik gives his half-smile.

'You wouldn't have been alone. It's a difficult game to play – talent spotting.'

'How do you discover new singers? Do you fly all over the place, or get tapes sent to you, or what?'

'Agents send out tapes of their latest clients. You hear talk of a new singer . . .'

'But when you are hearing a young voice for the first time, with its personality half formed, what is it that makes you sit up and say, "Now that is going to be a great singer!"?'

'It's a moment of recognition! You catch your breath. You know intuitively.'

'How often does that happen?'

'Not often enough. There are plenty of good singers about, but only a few great ones. I was particularly delighted to sign up both Jessye Norman and José Carreras, at the outset of their careers, on exclusive contracts for Philips soon after I joined the company in 1968. Jessye made her debut for us in *Le Nozze di Figaro* in 1970, and José in Verdi's *Un Giorno di Regno* at around the same time.

'Recently, the young Siberian baritone Dimitri Hvorostovsky touched me with his singing, just as José did when I first heard him. I am thrilled that I shall be producing Hvorostovsky's first opera recording.'

Erik doesn't wait for the next question, but starts telling me about working with Fritz Reiner on Verdi's Requiem.

'I was warned that he would be very difficult, but the truth was that he couldn't have been nicer. I think he saw me as a very young man and was rather protective of me – paternal.'

'That's the recording wih Leontyne Price and Jussi Björling?'

'Yes. But it wasn't supposed to be with Price. The New York office were mad keen on Leonie Rysanek at the time, but for some reason she had to drop out a few days before we were due to start recording. I phoned RCA, who had a contract with Decca then, in New York and got their permission to engage Leontyne, who I had met by chance in the Karntnerstrasse! Simionato was to be the mezzo, but she didn't know the part! We had to engage Rosalind Elias at short notice. She was very good.'

'Wasn't that Björling's last recording?'

'Yes. Both Jussi and Fritz Reiner died soon afterwards. A rather haunted recording.'

'During a recording session, how far can you go in challenging what singers have done? I mean the way they've phrased something, or their intonation.'

'Most singers are good professionals. They want to perform to the best of their ability, and they know that a recording is likely to be subjected to repeated scrutiny. Most respond well to a constructive challenge.'

'So could you have told Francisco Araisa, when you were recording *Il Barbiere di Siviglia*, that he was aspirating his runs?'

'I could have done.'

'Did you?'

'Do you think I should have done?'

'Well – ' It's my turn to hesitate.

'You've got to be practical. There is a limited time available. There are some things a singer can repeat to advantage. But making a radical alteration to a singer's technique is quite another matter. It might be asking too much of an artist who has sung a part dozens of times in one way to come into a studio and sing it quite differently. It just depends on the artist. One has to be pragmatic.

'I was recording *Il Barbiere* in Naples for Decca many years ago with the wonderful Teresa Berganza – I'll tell you this story because it means so much to me – and in her duet with Figaro, she had just reached 'Dunque io son . . . tu non m'inganni' when I knew we had to hear Rosina smile. I stopped the take and asked Berganza to try and smile with her voice at that moment. The next take, she did exactly that, and I used it in the finished recording. About twenty-five years later, I was listening to *Desert Island Discs* on the radio, and the guest chose exactly that moment to take to his desert island because of the way she smiled as she sang!

'In my Decca days, we often recorded with Del Monaco. We used to beg him to sing quietly. Sometimes he ignored our pleas completely. Other times, he'd manage to sing a couple of phrases quietly, then it was back to his old ways. His technique seemed to make it impossible for him to sing *piano* for any length of time. He could be thrilling, at Otello's first entrance, for instance. And he had a significant public following. But it was a wonderful relief when Bergonzi came in to replace him.'

'How much rehearsal time is there for an opera recording?'

'A couple of days' piano rehearsal? You seldom get the whole cast together at the same time.'

'The piano rehearsal is with the conductor, presumably?'

'Usually. Different conductors have different methods. Colin Davis asks the singers to feel and explore the emotions within the characters, especially the sexual tensions in a Mozart opera, for example. It's like method acting, I suppose. All very lively and entertaining, but, sadly, the process of converting, via technique, these ideas into a way of singing the roles to express such insights tends to take longer than the few days available for a recording. And some singers could never do it!'

'And what happens if the conductor's views differ radically from yours?'

'Maybe we've engaged the wrong conductor! No, that doesn't happen very often. I am concerned at what von Karajan did to some artists, encouraging them to sing parts for which their voices were not at all suited. Ricciarelli should never have sung *Turandot*, for instance. She had been recording roles more suited to her special talents for us, in *I due Foscari* and *La Bohème*, for example. But she was never a spinto, and I think her voice has suffered. Carreras also. Listen to that *Tosca* he recorded for us . . .'

'With Caballe and Colin Davis?'

'Yes. What a beautiful, lyric tenor you can hear in that

recording. Rhadames and Calaf require a different sort of tenor, surely?'

'But you've just recorded Carreras in *La Juive*. Isn't Eleazar a heavy, dramatic part for a tenor?'

'In the opera house it must be a killer because the great aria, 'Rachel, quand du Seigneur' comes after the best part of three hours, and immediately after a really tough duet! In the recording studio, the length of the piece is not a problem. And Eleazar does not require 'verismo' power. After all, it was created by Adolphe Nourrit, who sang Gluck and Rossini.'

'Erik, let's turn to one of today's rising stars, Cheryl Studer. She has already recorded Sieglinde, The Empress in *Die Frau Ohne Schatten*, and Elizabeth in *Tannhauser*. She is due to record Salome and Senta with Sinopoli . . .'

'. . . and the Queen of the Night for us!'

'Yes. And you've recorded her in *Guglielmo Tell* live at La Scala. I read somewhere that she's also singing Lucia! Isn't this a crazy schedule? When Suliotis burnt herself out, a great singer was lost. Isn't Studer in danger of the same fate?'

'Studer and Suliotis don't produce their voices in the same way. Studer doesn't sing recklessly. She is also a little older than Suliotis was at the time of *Nabucco*, and her voice is a more mature instrument.

'Nevertheless, even Olympic athletes in the peak of condition have to watch their fitness carefully. And singers on top of their form, as Cheryl Studer is at present, are well advised to do likewise.'

It's time for Erik to leave for the *Gramophone* Awards. We set out from his South Bank apartment and walk briskly towards Waterloo Bridge in delightful October sunshine. He chats about recording *Falstaff* with Bernstein and Fischer-Dieskau, a recent CD reissue that has given me much pleasure. I enthuse about the two Nielsen operas, *Maskarade* and *Saul and David*. How I wish Philips would record them both!

Then, halfway across the Thames, his pace slackens and he starts to tell me about Benjamin Britten, with whom he recorded

Peter Grimes, the *Spring Symphony* and *Serenade for Tenor, Horn and Strings*.

'There was a prickly, difficult side to Ben. He took offence very easily. Almost the last contact I had with him was in Vienna. Decca was recording at the Sofiensaal and Peter and Ben had dinner with us. They told us how they had just given a recital for the King of Greece, who had clearly been bored by the whole thing! Rather crossly, Ben added that after the recital, they had been seated at one of the lower tables for dinner. To make him feel a bit better about it, I turned to him and said; 'Just like Mozart!' Ben looked at me icily and said, "Thank you for putting me in my place, Erik." We hardly ever spoke again.'

Erik has stopped walking altogether to complete his story. I can tell that he is still hurt by this incident, even after many years. We shake hands and Erik skips down the steps to the Embankment and the Savoy Hotel, where his recording of the complete Mozart Piano Sonatas, with Mitsuko Uchida, has won the *Gramophone*'s top Instrumental Award.

November

After a year of planning, in which most of the work has been done by Andrew McKinnon and Max Roberts (Northern Stage Company and Live Theatre), the C. P. Taylor Festival has opened in Newcastle upon Tyne with productions of *Bandits* at Live Theatre's studio on the Quayside (and on tour in the region) and *Good* at the Playhouse. Bruvvers Theatre Company (based at Wallsend) is touring *Operation Elvis*, which can also be seen in a rival production organised and directed by actor Michael McNally as a lunchtime show in the Live Theatre studio. The region's leading amateur company, The People's Theatre, has *And a Nightingale Sang* in production, while the Northumberland Experimental Youth Theatre is performing *Peter Pan and Emily*. Tyne Tees Television has backed the Festival and is making a documentary for showing at Christmas in one of its local network slots.

The whole enterprise demonstrates the strengths and weaknesses of theatre in the North East. Very much to the region's credit have been the instant lines of communication between the various theatre companies, Northern Arts (the regional Arts Association), Tyne Tees Television, Northern Playwrights' Society, the local press and other interested bodies.

There has always been a tradition in the region of easy accessibility, which to an outsider looks very like a 'Geordie' mafia. When helping to start up Northern Playwrights' Society in the mid-seventies as an unknown and, worse still, not even a locally born playwright, I never had any problem in picking up the telephone, getting straight through to theatre directors, local politicians and business people, Newcastle's Head Librarian, Northern Arts, the local Press, or whoever I needed to contact, to arrange meetings or gather support for what I was trying to do. The C. P. Taylor Festival has shown that this spirit of welcoming and supporting initiative is still alive and flourishing in the North East.

The Festival was financed with £6,500 from Northern Arts, £3,000 from Tyne Tees Television, £1,000 from ABSA (a business sponsorship scheme funded by Central Government), and £1,000 from the City of Newcastle, who also provided plenty of support with advertising and publicity and other 'in kind' assistance.

Some months before the Festival started, Andrew McKinnon's Tyne Wear Theatre Company had to leave its base at the New Tyne Theatre, divorcing itself from the enthusiastic amateur company that owned the building. There was the very real possibility that the region's only resident (as opposed to touring) repertory company would vanish over night, together with its precious funding. It is to Andrew McKinnon's great credit that instead of seeking employment elsewhere, he regrouped as the Northern Stage Company, set up shop in new offices, and although without a permanent theatre in which to perform, carried on business as usual. As fate would have it, the first production of the newly formed company would be C. P. Taylor's *Good*, so the start of the Festival would also be the baptism of Andrew's company.

Not surprisingly, the quality of the various productions varied considerably. Live Theatre's *Bandits* was poorly designed and lit, even allowing for the minimally equipped studio and the demands of a touring set. The actors know each other's work, and that of director Max Roberts, too well and there was too much that was safe and routine to make the evening other than dutiful.

Good at the Playhouse was, by contrast, a triumph for all concerned. The audience knew the recent history of the company, of course, and was willing it every success. But Taylor's brilliant play is unusually difficult to perform, with a deluge of words and ideas to communicate, and a daring fluidity of structure. The evening took wing, making it among the most memorable in my experience, and reaffirming C. P. Taylor's talent (and, incredibly, there are still many doubters) in precisely the way such a Festival demands. David Roper's Halder, trying to retain cheerful rationality in the face of overwhelming horror, was unforgettable.

Working with no budget to speak of, and hiring Live Theatre's studio at his own expense, Michael McNally's production of *Operation Elvis* moved the entire audience to tears on the two occasions I saw it. The sight of the brain-damaged boy being hoisted into a boat to realise his dearest wish to float with his young friend on a Northumbrian lake was unbearably moving. The combination of suffering and ecstasy transformed the youngsters into living icons. I'm not sure whether 'Tears dripped off my chin!' on billboards outside the theatre would have packed out the house, but I confess willingly that they did, and I was not alone.

On the morning of the 'Gala Evening', I arrived on time at Live Theatre and started to rehearse an extract from *Lies about Vietnam* with 22-year-old Joe Caffrey. That evening he would be performing with Roy Marsden, who was travelling up from London with fellow actor Roger Kemp that afternoon.

Joe provides an interesting example of how a young actor on Tyneside can get started on a career. While still at school, he joined various Youth Theatres on North Tyneside (where he played one of the leads in an earlier production of *Bandits*) and demonstrated his enthusiasm and potential talent. The Education Authority then gave him a discretionary grant to go to LAMDA (London Academy of Music and Dramatic Arts). Max Roberts, who combines his role as Artistic Director of Live Theatre with work in youth theatres, was able to support Joe's grant application and to offer him his first professional contract. He made his debut in Phil Woods's adaptation of Jack Common's classic novel *Kiddars Luck*. Subsequently, Joe has worked with locally based Amber Films in Tom Hadaway's *In Fading Light*, done a season in pantomime at Newcastle's Theatre Royal, and has been cast in a lead part in Penny Woolcox's *Women in Tropical Places* for Film on Four International!

What this success story demonstrates, in addition to Joe Caffrey's personal ability, is the importance of funding and staffing youth theatres properly. Drama in schools, after the near acceptability in the sixties and seventies, is now harassed and sidelined. In Kent the budget for youth theatre has been axed entirely. Drama as part of the curriculum was always disliked by many teachers and reactionary educationists as being disruptive of school discipline, an abuse of space and resources and even a hotbed of anarchy!

By subsidising youth theatres outside of school time and premises, an Education Authority is providing an excuse for schools to regard Drama as being taken care of elsewhere and out of sight, which is appalling, but does provide common ground for enthusiastic and sometimes ambitious youngsters from all over the city to meet each other and work with professionals, which is splendid. However, it was never the intention of the Northumberland Experimental Youth Theatre, for example, to replace drama teaching within schools, but rather to be an adjunct to such teaching.

Also, the work done by youth theatres that are independent of schools is likely to be more performance and theatre orientated than Drama as part of a school curriculum. In the latter case, drama can be used as an active and practical teaching aid to all the other regular school subjects. Educational drama techniques can be most usefully employed in teaching History, Geography, English and Religious Education, and even the various sciences where cooperation with those departments is forthcoming. Sadly, my experience in the early seventies suggested that drama in schools was treated with the greatest antagonism by the small army of white coated science teachers, enthusiastically backed by the majority of senior staff, and I guess that their collective hand has been strengthened by the fierce trimming of budgets, and notions of the 'Core Curriculum', backed by legislation, that has been central to Conservative educational strategy.

Nevertheless, pioneering work in the North East was accomplished in the sixties by Northumberland Drama Officer Silas Harvey, and many of the Live Theatre Company actors are his graduates. The emergence of Joe Caffrey under the tutelage of Max Roberts and others is a testament to one aspect of the value of Silas's early work.

The C. P. Taylor Gala Evening itself was a long, funny, moving affair, with the unpredictable energy of spontaneity keeping everyone on their toes. As various speakers pointed out, Cecil, in life, would have been most embarrassed by such attention. But he would also have enjoyed it in his way, greeting again so many old friends and colleagues.

Cecil's son Avram concluded Part One of the evening by making an amusing speech about his father, and wishing his spirit a Happy Sixtieth Birthday. Cordelia Oliver, one time drama critic of the *Guardian* (and greatly missed in that role now) spoke of her conversations with Cecil in the early days of the Edinburgh Traverse Theatre, and testified to his sharp wit, while extracts from many plays were enlivened by splendid readings from a large company of actors.

Other playwrights present included Alan Plater, Tom Hadaway and Leonard Barras. Tyne Tees Television filmed the evening for their documentary about Cecil, and when his true stature is finally acknowledged internationally, their film record of performances and interviews is likely to be of great interest.

A number of characteristic C. P. Taylor themes were illustrated by juxtaposing extracts from so many different plays. These included the trivia of everyday domestic and personal problems set against the background of overwhelming and unchangeable historical events. Thus, in *Bread and Butter*, Morris, a Jew in Glasgow in the 1930s tries to defend Hitler's attitude towards German Jews, while wondering himself whether to agree to a traditional Jewish ceremony when he marries Sharon. In *Good*, Halder tries to cope with an increasingly dependent aged mother, and an affair with a student half his age, against the background of the rise of Nazi power.

Cecil repeatedly posed the question, 'How can people hope to change or influence the course of history when they are incapable of sorting out their most private and personal relationships?' Halder, in *Good*, finds himself swept along by events until he is left in charge of an extermination camp. Yet he appears more of a good man than an evil or wicked one.

In *Lies about Vietnam* (published by Methuen in *Gay Plays: 2*), the stormy homosexual relationship between an American airman (Tom) and his older British political activist lover (Cyril), threatens to divert them from their prime objective of changing public attitudes towards American aggression in Vietnam. The practical problems of occupying a hotel room in Newcastle, which is run by a homophobic landlord, seem greater than their historic political mission of holding an anti-American protest meeting in the City Hall.

Unknown to all of us at the Gala Evening was that at the very moment we were celebrating our late and sorely missed friend, the Berlin Wall was being torn down and Berliners of the East and West were dancing and singing in the streets. The irony of our private celebration of one man's achievement and the suddenness of twentieth century European history in the making would not have been lost on Cecil. He would have written a play about it.

After the hour's drive back home from Newcastle that evening, I got to bed at 2 am and couldn't sleep. Instead, I stayed up most of the night listening to the extraordinary news from Berlin on BBC radio's World Service. The reports were brilliantly managed and deeply moving.

It seemed imperative to get down to work on my new stage play for Live Theatre Company. I spent the next nine days writing about eighty pages of script and astonished (I hope!) Max Roberts and Andrew McKinnon by submitting my first draft to them two weeks before my 1 December deadline.

Green Fingers makes use of an untransmitted Granada Television *Crown Court* script. Whilst much of the action still takes place in the Crown Court, I have developed the storyline well beyond what was possible or required by Granada in the early eighties. About half the play takes place in various locations around Newcastle, rather than in the courtroom. Two young men are charged with an unremarkable burglary, but the story behind the offence is a curious one, and the issues, financial, political and personal, are far greater than the court realises.

In the present draft, much of the out of court material is sketched in, rather than fully developed. I will listen to the reaction of Max and Andrew, and any of the Live Theatre Company who want to talk about it, then, after letting the challenges and suggestions settle in my mind, I'll write a second draft which will, if things go well, transform the play into something unusual and interesting. That will be done in the first two weeks of January. Since I am likely to be flying to Canada for the *Tornrak* performances in Banff at the same time as *Green Fingers* goes into rehearsal in Newcastle, it is very important that Max Roberts has time to live with the script while I am still around to do rewrites.

Some playwrights prefer writing a new stage play with actors and a director on hand to hold improvisation sessions and impromptu read-throughs. Although I find it extremely useful to get challenges and reactions between drafts, I much prefer to do the writing on my own, and in my own time, rather than in the rehearsal room or with people leaning over my shoulder. A play is likely to be stronger for being one person's vision, rather than the result of a team effort. Writing for the stage does still provide the playwright with the opportunity for personal and idiosyncratic vision. The originality of film and television writing is too often corrupted by producers, directors and script editors, to say nothing of the power of the camera's lens, unrehearsed actors and a host of technicians. But for a playwright willing to write for small casts on tiny budgets and for minimal payment, theatre writing still allows considerable independence. However, no one should be surprised at the number of playwrights who are writing novels, where they can play director, designer, lighting expert and script writer simultaneously.

After three years of writing nothing but television and film scripts (most of which are still on the shelf!) it has been a relief to write something for the stage again. The technical problems of writing for a maximum of seven actors, which involves some complicated doubling and trebling of roles, has been fun, as has the challenge of writing extended, dialogue based scenes, which seldom have a place in screen writing.

The day before I completed the first draft, I got a call from John Cocker, who runs the Riverdale Hotel in Belligham, which specialises in entertaining touring cricket teams. One of their speakers had dropped out of their annual Dinner. Would I come and make a speech? Like an ass, I said yes!

I worked non-stop to complete *Green Fingers*, printed out one copy and sent it off to Max. In a state of exhausted euphoria, I prepared a ridiculously complicated speech, contrasting a season's cricket in the West Tyne League with the external pressures of personal and professional obligations, local tragedies and the amazing succession of world events that were busily re-writing the history books in Western Europe and China, and which were being brought nightly into our homes on television! It was the sort of scenario that C. P. Taylor might have chosen for a Film on Four International commission! In retrospect, the fragility of my mental state is all too obvious.

I arrived at the Riverdale Hotel, my head still spinning from completing the new play a few hours earlier, to find that the other speaker was none other than the great Jack Simmons! Also present were the former England player, Colin Milburn, and Wuzim Raja of Pakistan! And my speech was a disaster!

Oh God! As I sit here writing this, I scream and squirm at my performance! One of my recurring nightmares has been that I walk on to the platform at a packed Albert Hall ... there's a conductor and symphony orchestra waiting ... I sit down at the piano ... the orchestra starts some impossible concerto and I suddenly remember that I can't play the piano! My Riverdale speech was even worse than that!

As soon as I opened my mouth, I knew I had prepared entirely the wrong speech for that audience. Before I had completed my first sentence, I abandoned what I had prepared and tried to improvise. I blustered and spluttered. My head started to spin. Cold sweat dripped from my chin.

Maybe on another occasion I could have paddled my way through those tricky waters, but not in my present exhausted state. The play had drained my mental energy and I was helpless. Those present, most of whom had no reason to know me from Adam, could not know anything of my mental condition. They made their displeasure at my feeble efforts painfully, even unpleasantly, obvious. I was out of love with them and they with me, which considering that I should have been relaxing at home rather than stepping in at the last moment and making a fool of myself, seemed a little ungracious. But a big thank you to seventeen-year-old Grant Dunlop, a friend from Wark Cricket Club and waiting on the tables that evening, who stepped forward as soon as I sat down with a kindly word of support.

Jack Simmons saved the situation with a splendid speech, proving himself to be a kindly gentleman and a great professional, both on and off the field. I toughed out the remainder of the evening, apologising at once to John Cocker, my host, but not attempting to explain my failure.

Wuzim Raja came up to me afterwards in the bar.

'I'm Wuzim Raja, the Pakistan Test player,' he said, by way of introduction.

'Yes, I know.'

'Do you mind if I say something personal?' he asked.

'Say whatever you like,' I replied. Mercifully, I had been drinking Perrier water rather than alcohol.

'That was the worst speech I have ever heard!' he continued.

'Yes. I thought so too. I'm very sorry. A most embarrassing disaster.'

'And they say you're a writer?'

'Yes.'

'Have you ever sold any of your work?'

'Yes.'

'I'm really surprised to hear it!' said Wuzim.

'It surprises me sometimes too,' I said as cheerfully as I could.

'Why didn't you just shut up and sit down?'

'I should have done, shouldn't I. You learn from your mistakes, don't you, Wuzim?'

'I hope you do,' he added helpfully, making his own special contribution to Anglo-Pakistani relations.

We all grouped together for a photograph. Later, I thanked John Cocker for inviting me and slipped away, leaving whatever other merriments the night had in store for those with the inclination to pursue them.

My relationship with *Opera Now* seems to be going from bad to worse. Gwen Hughes has sent me further galleys of my first Erik Smith interview as re-drafted in dialogue format (presumably by her) which contains precisely none of the changes I requested previously! I have returned the proofs once more, with the changes clearly marked and a polite letter. What more can I do?

The interviews that I was asked by Antony to do with various contemporary librettists seem to have been shelved or passed on to someone else. My written request for more information remains unanswered. This is a great pity. I have particular qualifications for such an article. All I ask is that if I submit something that is not what the editors want, I should then be requested to re-write it until everyone is satisfied. That seems to me fair and professional.

As a playwright, rather than journalist, I need to know that if I interview a theatre director, or fellow writer, or producer, or anyone else, that what I write will not be edited or re-drafted without my knowledge. In the case of *Opera Now*, most of my articles have had textual changes that I have first encountered on opening the published magazine. In the case of the Erik Smith interview, the first knowledge that I had of the drastic revision was when the printed galleys were sent to me. The changes that I requested were all ignored. Now that I have requested these changes for the second time at the eleventh hour, I can only wait and see what appears in the February issue.

This matters to me. For better or for worse, it is my name that is published as the author of the article. It is quite simple to change the sense, or the tone of what has been written by altering a sentence here or there, or omitting the precise wording of a question and just printing the reply, or in many other ways. I'll go the scaffold for my own misdemeanours, if I must, but not for someone else's, if I can avoid it!

Erik Smith himself was extremely angry that copy he had worked on and authenticated with me should now be changed in this way. He phoned me to ask if I could do anything to stop the editorialised article being printed. I thought it was unlikely, after the angry reception to my previous and repeated protests. I apologised unreservedly for what had happened.

'Goodbye, Michael!' said Erik, with a finality that suggested that he never wanted to hear my name ever again. I was left holding a dead phone.

Shortly after leaving teaching, I found it necessary to leave my rented cottage and move into Newcastle. I had very little money and from 1 May 1974 had no regular income. I rented a room in Jesmond (north of the city centre) for £4.50 a week and set up shop.

The £100 that I was paid for my first professionally produced play was therefore of the greatest importance. It was given the title *The Boy who cried Stop!* by its director, Jan Sargent, and concerned a boy who didn't much like his parents or his immediate world of school and the streets. He found that by shouting 'Stop!' at the top of his voice he could enter his fantasy world as though it was real.

After encounters and adventures with a handful of zany characters, including a Pirate, Cat Lady and a Clown called Knockabout, he finds his secret world is even more alarming than the one he has left, so he scurries back home!

My script worked and the thousands of eight- and nine-year-olds that saw it enjoyed it. Precisely how the staff coped with their children rushing around shouting 'Stop!' at the tops of their voices after we had all packed the set away in the van, we were never around long enough to discover.

The production lasted for eight weeks, which is still the longest run in this country of any play I have written. And for me, the experience was invaluable. Attending my first 'read through', getting to know the company, and trying to face up to a barrage of script 'challenges' was both exciting and bewildering.

One of the hardest things for an inexperienced writer is to know whether what you have written is going to be any good in performance. Lines may read sensibly in your head, or even off the page at a read through, but what happens when actors are performing 'off the book' is another matter.

There is a world of difference between theatrical dialogue and the dialogue tradition of short stories and novels. And it is the latter form of dialogue that some inexperienced dramatists employ, to stultifying effect.

There are also many structural practicalities to consider. Has an actor got enough time to change a costume? Have you engaged the audience's attention from the start? Does it flag in the middle? What is a satisfactory ending, anyway? Is your script all story with shallow characters in the manner of countless television scripts? Or are your detailed characters stranded in a static narrative?

On television the power of the camera is so great that characters can achieve personality with a minimum of dialogue. A poor script can be dressed up to look good on film.

In the theatre, the dramatist's talent is exposed more ruthlessly. In the early stages of rehearsal, the actors know that there is still time for script changes and re-writes. They are likely to come off the book in the second week and by that time they are stuck with what they've got, warts and all. So it is not surprising that the playwright can be given a rough ride during that first week.

Crucial and rapid decisions have to be made. Is it an actor problem? A director or company problem? Or a script problem? How difficult it is for a playwright to know for sure. How tempting to make an ass of oneself and stubbornly defend the indefensible!

A playwright's rehearsal checklist might include the following:

1. Make sure that the script at the read-through is as far advanced as possible.
2. Don't expect the company to give a performance of your play from the outset. Remember that actors perform with the text in their heads, not their hands. And, like the rest of us, there is no reason why an actor should be a good reader.
3. Don't interrupt or interfere. Let the director and the actors get on with it. Wait until you are asked a specific question if you possibly can. Let the director do the directing.
4. Even if you do manage to keep your mouth shut, watch out for negative body language! Don't hold your head in your hands, or groan, or keep crossing and uncrossing your legs! The actors are very aware of your presence and need encouragement and support, not a knee in the groin!
5. Try to resist the temptation to give 'notes' (I mean of a professional variety) to the actors. Always work through the director.
6. Spend some time with the company outside rehearsal

times (maybe during the lunch break, for example), but don't over do it. The actors need time to themselves, and from read through to first night seems like a lifetime of experience in which privacy is at a premium.

7. Don't smoke in the rehearsal room, even if one or two of the actors do. Two thirds of those present will hate the foul air, and keeping the actors' voices in good shape is crucial. Instead, take in a couple of packets of Polo mints each day, which soothe the throat and are fun to share around.

8. If you face a crisis over the text, with an actor (or, for Heaven's sake, the entire company!) wanting to change something, don't be stubborn. Try out new suggestions and different ideas. Re-write lines and see if they work better. Sometimes, the actor's idea is better than yours. Sometimes, the company will discover that your version of the text is indeed the best. In short, keep your head. Be reasonable. Be flexible. Remember the motto you should have stuck on your word processor, 'Try it and see!'

9. Don't drink alcohol at lunchtime. If you do, you're bound to say something really stupid in the afternoon session!

10. Remember the company doesn't just consist of actors. Be respectful, polite, understanding and helpful to everyone connected with the production. Get to know the names of everyone. And don't forget the people you don't generally meet. I mean the wardrobe department, the electricians, the switchboard operator, the box office personnel and so on. And on the opening night, send each a card to thank them and wish them luck. Don't leave anyone out!

Wonderful! The vocal score of *Tornrak* has just arrived from Canada. John Metcalf's name appears on the score, but mine not at all.

December

It is, of course, a depressing month. A time of crowded shops, frantic efforts to send a hundred Christmas cards, and the pressure of where to spend Christmas itself. If only there was a way of leaving it all behind. Most years, I travel down to London for a couple of days and then go on to join my mother, brothers and sister, and their wives and children, at Westcliff-on-Sea. I become Uncle Mickey (how I hate that cute hangover from childhood) and am on call twenty-four hours a day to play table tennis, squash, indoor cricket with Antony, Denys, Emma, William, John, Mark and Sally, and anyone else who wants to join in the fun.

I do love them all, and I don't doubt that I'll look back on these once a year family occasions with pleasure, dread and sadness. I'll try to forget the appalling Christmas show of *Wind in the Willows* at the local theatre that Denys and I sneaked out of at the first interval. Paying out £15 to witness the vandalising of a beautiful story isn't my idea of a Christmas treat.

Family foursomes at table tennis was better value. William and I versus John and Antony (or was it the other way round?) with lots of laughter and scandalous verbal abuse. Brisk walks along the sea front to Southend and an endless round of turkey based lunches and dinners punctuate the routine. No one wants to eat as much, or see as many people. People who haven't seen each other since last Christmas soon run out of things they want to say.

My sister, Sally, and I are both single. I have, in the past, felt a sense of externally imposed failure at Christmas, not having a family of my own. If Sally feels the same way, she never mentions it. But we don't discuss personal matters in our family. We show our affection for each other obliquely. We all kiss my mother on the cheek, but that is the limit of our physical contact. Brothers wouldn't be seen dead embracing brothers. Fifteen years ago I was besieged with 'When are YOU going to get married, Mickey?' and would get angry and say, 'You're so bloody thick! I'm never going to get married! I'm telling you now! I'm never going to, so stop asking me such dumb questions!' In our family, it would be unthinkable to be more specific than that. I haven't been asked a single question about my personal life, or its relationships, for more than a decade.

When it comes to my plays, my family loves *Lent* but is circumspect about everything else, although curious about what I am doing next. Neither of my brothers has seen *Rents*, nor do they intend to see it. John was horrified when my friend and trusty supporter, Christopher Dunham, directed a production of *Rents* at the Palace Theatre, Westcliff, just round the corner from Alleyn Court. Brothers John and Mark will inherit part of the royalties from the play, if I get run over by a bus. They'll take a closer interest in it then.

My family stays away from first nights, preferring to see a performance later in the run, if at all, when I am not around. This is not because they don't care. It's just embarrassing to see me unburdening myself in public, when we never behave like that in private.

Moving as far away from my family as possible was an important factor in achieving independence. Northumberland may as well be in a different country. And with my isolated cottage as home base, I can get on with my life and my work without harassment, however well intentioned. Better the outlaw in the hills than the sheriff in the town.

As well as joining in all family events as required, I managed to listen to all nine Bruckner symphonies, conducted by Eugen Jochum, on my portable CD player, as well as cello sonatas by Martinu and all the symphonies of Tippett in the space of four days!

Throughout the month, the most extraordinary events in Eastern Europe have been unfolding on television like fiction. On Christmas Day we watched the President of Romania and his wife clamber out of a tank, where they had been held prisoner, given a brief medical examination, condemned and shot by a firing squad. It was the medical examination that was odd. How many dramatists would have thought of that?

The day after Boxing Day, as soon as the trains were running again, I packed up my rucksack and headed northwards, easily resisting the temptation to stop off in London. To be on my own again, an adult independent and free, was a huge relief. The crowded trains were full of happy, single people who looked as though Her Majesty's pleasure had granted clemency. I saw a young man in search of a seat and waved to him to join me. He was a student doctor who talked of films, Hi-Fi and tropical illnesses. I ate one of his sandwiches then we settled down contentedly to read our books.

At Haltwhistle Station, late in the afternoon, it was growing dark. Mercifully, it wasn't raining so the four-mile hike up to my cottage wasn't too much of an ordeal. Instead of taking the shortest route by road, I decided to take the footpath through the woods from Bellister to Burnfoot Farm. The dead of winter crowded round my head, trying to break in. For over a week there had been nothing but the noise of trains, cars and thousands of people. Stillness, punctuated by my soft footfall, reclaimed its usurped kingdom. My shirt became soaked with sweat behind my backpack. I thought of the fire I'd light, the hot bath and music.

'What was his name? The one that drowned himself. You mind him?'

Coulson Teasdale of Kellah Farm, father of Tom, is at my neighbours' house, Pat and John Phillipson, with a handful of other locals. It is New Year's Eve and I am in a black mood.

'He had four sons. He left his coat by the burn and drowned himself. There was a note in his pocket and four oranges.'

'One for each son?' said Pat.

'Aye.'

'He was a strange 'un.'

'Aye. He was that.'

'It was sad, like . . .'

'Aye.'

'Who was it that found him?'

'Now then . . . I cannot mind that, now,' said Coulson thoughtfully. It was his story and even those that knew about it waited for Coulson to finish. 'Sad . . . very sad . . .'

A murmur of agreement.

An hour later, I walked home thinking of that poor man and his children and their tragic gift of oranges. It was a country tale straight out of Brothers Grimm. I was sure that each son would react differently to his orange, triggering triumph, disaster or magic.

I booted up the computer, loaded *Green Fingers* and wrote the concluding three scenes of the play, incorporating the story of the suicide's oranges. In my story, young David Benson has been brought up in a children's home without knowing who his true parents really were. Behind his love of a crooked street trader and his passion for horticulture, would be an orange that would lead him to his natural mother.

1990 crept in as I wrote without songs or whisky. I finished the new draft at two in the morning. An occasional 'first footer' drove past my house, none stopping. As the ashes of the bonfire at Allendale cooled off in the neighbouring valley, I watched silently as the dot matrix printer chattered out my new play.

Postscript

The auditioning and casting for *Green Fingers* was done by director Max Roberts, with help from Andrew McKinnon of Northern Stage Company. Casting the première production of a play is especially important and the playwright should be welcome to sit in on auditions. For practical reasons, this is not always possible. In my case, living in the far north of England when auditions are generally held in London, has meant that I often let the director get on with it. It may be that there is a clause in the playwright's contract giving him or her the right of casting approval and the right to attend all auditions and rehearsals. (The more 'rights' you can work into your contract the better, even if you seldom have need to resort to them.) I was delighted that three outstanding actors from the North East, Michael McNally (who was in the Film on Four *Accounts*), Donald McBride and Colin MacLachlan, were all free to be cast. Peter Peverley, whom I had seen in *Operation Elvis* during the C. P. Taylor Festival looked ideal for the 21-year-old trainee gardener, David Benson. Peter would be making his professional debut and getting his Equity card. Scottish actor Roy Hanlon, with whom I'd worked at STV and who has appeared in over three hundred television dramas, would make a wonderful Judge Partington-Jones. Max went down to London to find the Prosecution and Defence Counsels, and returned with Ian Oliver and Hilary Dawson, neither of whom I knew.

Because of my trip to Canada for *Tornrak*, which was during the *Green Fingers* rehearsal period, it was doubly important for Max and I to check through the script before rehearsals started. He came out to my cottage for the day. We read through the latest draft of the script out loud, discussing and noting all changes and re-writes on the way. I also had the script checked once again by a barrister for technical correctness, and was able to emphasise and explain the reasons why particular forms of words were used at various moments of the trial. It was essential that nothing should be changed during rehearsals that might undermine the authenticity of courtroom procedure.

At the end of a long session, I entered all the edits and re-writes onto floppy disk and printed out yet another draft of the script, while Max, who has suddenly developed an appetite for opera, listened for the first time to Pavarotti singing 'Nessun Dorma', Callas singing lots of things, and the Björling/Merrill *Pearl Fishers* duet.

A parcel delivery van has drawn up outside my house. I go out to investigate. It's a package for my neighbour, but he isn't at home, so I accept and sign for the delivery. The driver, whom I've never met before, wants to talk. He sees that I'm a listener and soon starts to tell me some of his life's adventures.

'I come from Eastern Europe. Originally I do. I'm British now. For two months. I came here in the fifties, of course.'

'You came from Hungary?' I'm guessing.

'Yes! How you know? Hungary . . .'

'I was in Budapest in 1966.'

'You were?'

'We were taken to the official camp site and I went to the washroom and was immediately approached by a student wanting to exchange forints for pounds or dollars.'

'I tell you, I am not surprised.'

He starts to roll a cigarette, like a thin straw.

'You know, I was arrested and sent to the Ukraine.'

'What for?'

'I was in the army – the Hungarian army – anyway, my father was in the pub one night and he said to his friend, "Look at this!" and showed one of my pay slips, and it was a very little amount of money, I can tell you! But someone overheard. Later, two Russian soldiers came to our house. I answered the door and they wanted to arrest my father. I thought it was a joke at first. Then my dog bit the soldier and my mother screamed and fainted and the other soldier shot the dog and I was arrested. They put sixty of us in a transit lorry. There was one metal drum for us to use as a lavatory. We washed it out each morning with soap and water and they served our food out of the same drum! But when we reached the Ukraine, the local people surrounded the lorry and the Russian soldiers ran away and we were all free! My God! We were scampering off in all directions like rabbits! I found my way back to Hungary and rejoined my unit. What else could I do?

'Then, when the Russians invaded, I was in a tank and the tank, it was hit, direct. My four friends were killed and I was more than half dead. Very lucky for me, I was flown out of Hungary to Britain. I had my ribs sticking out of my chest! I remember someone squeezing a lemon into my mouth ... and the juice ... swallowing it. Then nothing! Then I marry a girl from Carlisle and have a family! And here I am at your door!

'My daughter is mad. She goes with her boyfriend to the Costa del Sol. I say "Go to Blackpool. It's all there! No need to go to Spain!" but they go. What am I to do?

'Now I am British citizen, I am no longer a security risk. I take parcels to Army Camps and MOD and before they stop me at the gates and take my parcels there. For years they do this. Now I am British, they wave me through and in I go! Before – I tell you this – before, if I had an Irish passport in one hand and a bomb under my armpit, they wave me through because I have an Irish passport! But because I am an honest Hungarian, they stop me! It's called Security!

'And I hate the Poll Tax! You British look after your old people very badly. Worse than anywhere! Now I can vote, who should I vote for? Not bloody Thatcher, that's for sure. Not bloody

Kinnock either. You know what Kinnock do if he gets in? The first thing! He give independence to Wales. You see! I know it. The stupid sod! All sorts of trouble if Kinnock is in. I think I vote Green. Good idea? A Green Hungarian from Carlisle? I seen too much of politicians in my life.'

He lights the butt of his cigarette and it vanishes into ash.

'Now I must go! Many miles to drive. Goodbye, my friend.'

I take the parcel indoors as he drives away.

At the end of the first week of *Green Fingers* rehearsals, I flew off to Canada for the two preview performances of *Tornrak* at the Banff Centre. *Opera Now* asked me to keep a diary record of the experience.

Wednesday 14 February

'Everyone has an original template . . . you know . . . beneath all the mess of life. If I can get back to that, so many problems can be solved.'

My neighbour on the Wardair flight from Gatwick to Calgary is a chiropractor from Victoria, BC. As she speaks, I am thinking of tornraks, guardian spirits of Inuk culture.

'But what if the original template of one of your patients turns out to be that of a serial killer? If you turn a kleptomaniac into a murderer, have you done a good job?'

The in-flight movie is *Turner and Hooch*, a feeble story of a simple-minded cop and an ugly dog, a tornrak made flesh.

I am met at Calgary by Luc, who drives me to The Banff Centre at the northern end of the Rockies like an angel of Death, speeding through ice and snow and enthusing about the Canadian film, *Jesus of Montreal*.

A quick shower and then straight into rehearsals in the thousand seater theatre, where director Mike Ashman is running the Arctic scenes of Act One. I am blinking with tiredness as Milak, an Inuit (eskimo) girl saves the shipwrecked Arthur Nesbit from North Shields from an attack by a polar bear. In the fight that follows, the bear is harpooned to death. A chorus of Inuit Spirit hunters pays homage to the dying creature. Milak skins it and the spirit of the bear is released. It wanders across the arctic tundra, throat singing in little rhythmic gasps.

Designer Bernard Culshaw, with whom I last worked on *Massage* at the Lyric, Hammersmith, greets me in the darkness. His arctic sets have the roundness and vestigial lines of Inuit sculpture. He wants to know if I've heard any cricket scores.

Thursday 15th

The first orchestral playthrough of Act Two. The orchestra consists of resident Banff Centre artists and a few extra musicians from Calgary. The conductor is Peter Stanger who issues a brief admonishment to the bemused wind section, who are struggling to sight-read John Metcalf's tricky music. I sit next to John, who is poring over his thick orchestral score. We started work on *Tornrak* in 1986 and this is the first time either of us have heard Act Two with the full orchestral forces.

As the drama of Milak's experiences in Britain unfolds, I am moved to tears a couple of times. It's the 1850s and she has been 'rescued' with Arthur, only to end up being displayed in a travelling fair as 'The Savage Woman of the Frozen North'. She escapes, with the aid of a Dancing Bear, and after living wild in the Welsh Mountains, travels northwards in an attempt to get home. She cannot understand how people who live in a land with undreamed of resources can ignore rampant poverty and starving children. She uses her skills as a hunter to kill sheep, is arrested and condemned to death.

It's staggeringly cold ouside, −25C. Moving between the buildings leaves me gasping. Every time you breathe in, ice forms inside your nostrils, and when you breathe out, it melts!

More rehearsals of the Arctic scenes in the afternoon (piano only). Milak's tornrak, a White Owl, flies about the darkened stage like a pair of silk knickers! How thin is the line between the wonderful and the absurd. Mike Ashman waves to me cheerily.

Friday 16th

Lighting rehearsal in the morning. Good! I can go off in search of fun and adventure! It's now −35C outside, which doesn't help. I discover a hunky lumberjack playing alone on the squash court. Just what I'm looking for. Yes, he'd love to play.

More problems with the Arctic scenes in the afternoon. Milak sings entirely in Inuktitut during Act One. Most of the time you can figure out what is happening, but I wonder if it wouldn't be better if she sang her inner thoughts in English, while speaking to Arthur in Inuktitut. How are the audience expected to know where she has come from, and the strange dream she has had about 'the bird with many wings' that is going to carry her off in its claws? If the only way of understanding this is from the programme synopsis, haven't we failed to do our job properly?

There is a run with piano of both Acts in the evening. In the interval, John Metcalf and I go off for a beer. John is very concerned at the ragged state of the production. I try to reassure him, but with little success.

Act Two doesn't look much better and John puts on a brave public face. I'm a little less worried, knowing how much work is done on a production in the last few days.

Saturday 17th

There's another technical rehearsal, so I slip off to the library where there is a splendid collection of opera recordings on LP and CD and the necessary equipment and headphones. I listen to the 1950s live recording of *Alcina* with Sutherland and Wunderlich, conducted by Leitner. Very collectable and in reasonable sound. Then it's more squash with Rob.

The orchestra joins the company for Act One in the theatre for the first time. I am knocked out by the beauty of John's opening scene, and the foreboding he creates. What a marvellous start to a mariner's yarn. The experience offers some comfort after the torture of the previous evening. The Polar Bear costume changes on every appearance.

Our Inuk adviser is Francis Piugattuk. In a bout of homesickness that evening, he runs up Tunnel Mountain in the dark. He arrives back in the bar to tell us what he has just done. 'I found some hard snow!' he announces with delight. He has stood on the real world for a while to regain his strength. 'I think I'd like to stay on at Banff to see the next production after *Tornrak* if they'll have me.' Francis has never worked in a theatre before. He has made two harpoons and an Inuit drum for the opera, each being a work of art in its own right.

Sunday 18th

Wonderful! A day off! I discover *Susanna's Secret* (the opera by Wolf-Ferrari) in the library, with Scotto and Bruson, and with the wonderful Sir John Pritchard conducting.

More squash with Rob, who turns out not to be a lumberjack at all, but another aspiring playwright! Oh well . . .

It's getting warmer! Only about −10C! Canadian tenor Christian Jensen drives me to Lake Louise, which is frozen over and surrounded by stunning mountains. At one end is a vast hotel and at the other, a glacier. Chris and I walk as far as we can, watch an idiot risking his life ice climbing without a rope and have a close encounter with a porcupine. It wanders, unconcerned at our presence, on its way. It looks me in the eye. It must be my tornrak. 'Is that what I'm like?' I ask Chris. 'When I see your tail flip up and get stuck with a bunch of quills, I'll let you know!'

Monday 19th

I discover an astonishing recording of Jussi Björling when he was nine years old (1920). It is easily recognisable as the voice it was to become and to encounter young Jussi singing his heart out is a most moving experience (Bluebell ABCD 016).

In the afternoon it's Act Two with orchestra. Very slow going. Lots of stops and technical hitches. For the first time, director Mike Ashman is showing signs of stress. The lighting has become over elaborate, creating problems for the brilliant Michael Whitfield. I want to change some of the text, especially the un-Victorian expletives that John has a fondness for. 'Lousy bastard!' doesn't sound like Victorian abuse to me. Replacement suggestions include 'Heathen bastard!' and 'Damned heathen!' which sound like comic strip jargon. John's 'Stow it!' and 'Pigeon brain!' get by, but since bad language is so unusual in Victorian literature, anything, even if it is authentic, sounds anachronistic. 'Bloody' sounds wrong, but isn't.

Dreadful sore throat! I go to bed at 7 pm feeling like death.

Tuesday 20th

Uncomfortable night. Heavy cold developing. I'm back at work, but try to avoid getting too close to the singers. Messy piano run of Act One in the afternoon. John Metcalf takes me into his office and expresses his concern. Only two more working days before opening, and so much needs doing!

I slip off for a sauna, feeling rotten. My nose bleeds profusely. I buy aspirins and listen to *Intermezzo* with Lucia Popp in stunning form.

That evening, the first of two dress rehearsals goes better than expected. But in the Arctic scenes, Arthur is dressed only in his sailor outfit. I don't get any impression of the coldness of the place, and Heaven knows, we've had plenty of opportunity to find out what being cold feels like!

I'm far from convinced by the ending, when Milak, in the form of her White Owl tornrak swoops down to release Arthur's spirit as he freezes to death at the ship's wheel. Instead of letting Milak sing, John has written a load of owl-like shrieks, which might work eventually, but are laughable at the moment. But I'm all for taking risks, and there are plenty in *Tornrak*! Fides Krucker gives a committed performance as Milak, brilliantly acted and full of detail. Christopher King's Arthur is strongly sung, and he looks splendid. Of the Canadian cast, only Richard E. Armstrong, an extended voice specialist, is also in the WNO production. He plays both bears and old Utak, and has the distinction of dying three times in the course of the evening!

Aspirins and bed.

Wednesday 21st

It's thawing outside! In three days the temperature has risen by 40C! I go for a walk to get some fresh air into my body. The elk are taking full advantage of the extra food revealed by the change of weather and are wandering everywhere, fearlessly.

The final dress rehearsal goes quite well, but I am still bothered by the ending, which doesn't have the climactic resolution the opera surely requires. Milak's shrieks sound more like clucks. Bernard Culshaw wanders up in the dark, mumbling something about Milak laying an egg!

I try to quell a laugh and my nose bleeds again!

Thursday 22nd

A whole day off! The WNO gang starts to arrive (immediately christened 'The Taffia' by the Canadians!). Conductor Richard Armstrong (not to be confused with the singer/actor of the same name) arrives and we go for a long walk along the Bow River to the Banff Springs Hotel. He has been conducting *Ariadne auf Naxos* in Frankfurt and raves about the Bacchus of American tenor Michael Sylvester. 'Sensational! It's an impossible role, but he sang it with ease. Staggering!' Richard also talks of the first time he heard the Siberian baritone Dmitri Hvorostovsky during the Cardiff Singer of the World competition. 'It was the end of a long day and the orchestra was tired. Dmitri came on and sang an aria from *Macbeth*. At the end, the players put down their instruments and gave him a spontaneous ovation! An unforgettable moment!'

Friday 23rd

The day of the first public performance! It's warm and sunny. My cold is much better and I'm feeling full of energy again.

Brian McMaster, WNO Managing Director, arrives from Vancouver. Various luminaries from opera companies all over Canada are flying in.

More long walks on my own. I buy first night cards and visit a Native American Museum. Before the performance, there is a hot meal and a welcoming drink for the new arrivals at the house of Banff Centre President Paul Fleck.

The performance goes quite well and is politely received. No one tells me about the 'walk down' at the end, and I am left on my seat in the auditorium while everyone else takes a bow. I applaud enthusiastically.

Saturday 24th

I need to blow off a lot of steam! Long walk in the morning with Harvey Chusid of *Opera Canada* magazine. He would have preferred to see the entire opera with surtitles! 'Even the English bits?' I ask with surprise. Yes! I tell him how I hate surtitles in the theatre, although I don't mind subtitles for opera on television.

After lunch, it's off to the naturally heated sulphur pools with Mark Morris (son of Jan) and gang. I love floating around in the hot water out of doors in the cold air, and smelling faintly of bad eggs!

Mark is another librettist, and has had a recent success with *The Skin Drum* in collaboration with British composer Julian Grant. We discuss the librettist's lot and both feel undervalued and underpaid. (My fee for *Tornrak* was a meagre £1,000! Or, if you prefer, £250 a year for the four years the project has taken!) In addition to the embarrassment of the unintentional muddle over the 'walk down', I received precisely NO first night cards from anyone. Thanks a lot!

Then it's up to the top of Sulphur Mountain in the gondola! Joanna Baker, Head of WNO marketing, and I slip and slide across hazardous ridges of snow to the highest observation point and gaze in wonder at the world beneath us. We all walk back the four miles to the Banff Centre inventing the scurrilous adventures of 'The Two Bad Boys and the Wicked Queen of the Woods' as our contribution to Canadian culture for the afternoon. No chance of a bear attack with our racket going on!

The final performance goes splendidly. The audience loved it! One five-year-old boy has been to two dress rehearsals and the two performances that week. He is an authority on *Tornrak* and explains the complexity and wonder of the story to anyone within earshot.

The day after flying back to London, I was on the train to Newcastle for the World Premiere performance of *Green Fingers*. I decided not to go to the final dress rehearsal. The company would not be used to having me there and I thought it would be better for me to show my trust and confidence in them by staying away until the official opening.

Meanwhile, the *Journal*, the North East's daily newspaper, published a half-page story about me, with four photographs, under the banner 'PLAYWRIGHT WHO PLAYS A CAPTAIN'S INNINGS'. The article by David Issacs was accurate in detail and flattering. It was keenly and explicitly concerned about my homosexuality, suggesting that I was Britain's leading gay playwright! (I can think of at least a dozen more eminent dramatists than myself who might have something to say about that!)

Although my nature was no secret, in the way of things in the country, such matters are generally known but not mentioned. I knew that the article was being widely read and discussed in Haltwhistle and its honest bluntness (which delighted me) would embarrass some local people. So I grabbed my red shopping bag and went to Haltwhistle, buying something in all my usual shops and saying good morning to everyone, showing my unashamed face everywhere.

The reaction was interesting, ranging from one or two people who crossed the street rather than walk past me to those who went out of their way to greet me. A couple of lads shouted over to me, 'Good article this morning, Mike. When does the play open?' A number of the good ladies of the town stopped to chat in a public demonstration of support. A car screeched to a halt and Janice Hepple, Haltwhistle's number one women's squash player shouted over to ask if I wanted a game that afternoon. And so it went on.

It was, I believe, a significant day. I'd be surprised if there was an extended family in town that did not have at least one gay person in it. Yet such matters have always been treated in a secret, private way which fuelled shame and fear. My own publicity wasn't going to change all that overnight, but it was a step in the right direction and brought a measure of relief and delight to more people locally than some would like to admit. There followed the predictable phonecalls, often from people unwilling to give their names, who wanted someone to talk to. I am used to that and help if I can.

And, joy of joys, *Green Fingers* opened splendidly! A partisan audience laughed noisily at every bit of fun and shouted its approval at the end. The local reviews were excellent and within a few days the ten scheduled performances were well booked.

I was astonished at how many people travelled great distances to see the play. Peter James came up from the Lyric, Hammersmith, Peter Lichtenfels came up from the Leicester Haymarket (only to return to find his contract terminated!), and other notables came from London's Royal National Theatre, from Edinburgh, Glasgow, Manchester and elsewhere. In its brief run, *Green Fingers* was an event. Various commercial interests also had a look at it. In the end, it was none other than Michael Codron, who had declined to commission a new play from me a year earlier, who read it and loved it and wanted to put it on. Within days, he had joined forces with Dan Crawford of The King's Head (a pub theatre venue in London with an outstanding track record) and Andrew McKinnon of the Northern Stage Company. As I write, the plan is to mount a new production at The King's Head before the end of the year with a notable cast all set to transfer into the London West End if the omens are right.

So my new stage play, which took (like *Lent* some years previously) just a couple of weeks to write, has wings. I'm keeping my own green fingers crossed!

Then, of course, there is the new cricket season to prepare for. Haltwhistle, as West Tyne League champions, are on a high, and pre-season nets have been well attended. The early spring weather has been unusually warm and sunny. My back, which has given me lots of problems in the past few years, seemed to be holding together until I tried to shift my grass cutter up a bank. Then it snapped again, providing me with a few weeks of discomfort. I have played in the first few games with mixed fortune.

I was a bit unlucky a couple of games ago. Before I was off the mark, a ball pitched just short of a length outside the off stump. My bat was well up, ready to cut, when the ball shot up and moved into my body. (Bloody wicket!) I decided not to play it, moved my bat behind my head, but the damned ball just followed me round, touching the tip of my bat and giving an easy catch to the wicket keeper. Wilcox out for a duck, to the great delight of the opposition! What I should have done is lift the bat well above my head, rather than behind it. Bowler Alan Armstrong of Allendale, for whom I have the greatest respect, was still gloating when I came in to umpire.

'Best ball of the season!' he grinned.

'My arse!' I grumped.

It's down to London, then over to Cardiff for a public symposium on *Tornrak*, to be recorded by BBC Radio for the interval of the forthcoming broadcast of the opera.

An hour before the symposium, WNO Finance Director, Adrian Trickey, asked me into his office and closed the door. Grim faced, he said that someone called Paul Swift had been on the phone to protest that his play had been used without his permission. Apparently, he had written the TIE programme that John Metcalf had seen four years earlier. I had never heard of Paul Swift, although I had seen a transcript of his programme. I had assumed (wrongly as it turned out) that John had got the approval of the TIE company to show me their work. I suggested to Adrian that it was John he should be talking to and not me. I had been commissioned to write the opera libretto in good faith. It was up to those responsible for the commission to check that any external rights were correctly cleared. Anyway, Milak's story was based on the true story of Mikak. Arthur Nesbit from North Shields was my invention (the TIE company's Arthur was a fourteen-year-old cabin boy) and the rest of the narrative was, as far as I was aware, my own invention.

Nevertheless, I made it clear to Adrian that if fellow writer, Paul Swift, had in any way been mistreated, I would certainly support any reasonable and rightful claim he might have.

I saw John Metcalf briefly before we entered the auditorium for the symposium.

'Surely you sorted this matter out correctly with Paul Swift four years ago?' I muttered.

John was noncommital, but suggested that he didn't see Paul Swift's claim as a serious problem. But I felt a sinking, wretched feeling in my stomach, resenting that my own professional integrity should appear tarnished. Clearly, this was a matter that should be settled fairly and reasonably as soon as possible.

As soon as I got back to London the next morning, I went to see Joy Westendarp. I was sure we should contact Paul Swift at once to determine the true facts of the matter. I was relieved to hear that she had already done precisely that the previous evening and that the first steps in untangling what might become a most tedious knot had been taken. How marvellous and invaluable Joy is, both in fair weather and in foul.

On the opening night, my family came in droves, with my brother John driving them in the Alleyn Court minibus. I even got a bunch of first night cards! They will end up in my scrapbook (volume 9), along with all the press reviews and published articles on *Tornrak*.

I was on my best behaviour, drinking only orange and lemonade to stop me slurring my speech and shooting my mouth off. The performance went very well, with Penelope Walker and David Owen singing and acting excellently as Milak and Arthur. The audience received the opera with great enthusiasm. I even got to take a bow this time!

The WNO chorus's name for the opera is *No No Nanook*!

The next morning, after the party, it was off to Birmingham by car, with John Metcalf, Keith Turnbull (dramaturge) and lecturer John Waterhouse to speak at a day school on the opera at Birmingham University.

Then, the day after that, back to London, and a meeting at the British Medical Association. John Dawson wants me to script three short films on cancer and sudden death, which, after what I have been through in the past few days, seems entirely appropriate!

Then ... at last ... back north and home again.

There is a rush of new work coming in. As well as the three BMA films ('Can we have treatments next week, please?') there is an episode of a new thriller series, *Harry Gamble*, a detective on board the Queen Mary in the 1930s. And I have just had a call from Michael Darlow to see if I am interested in scripting the first volume of Sir Denis Forman's autobiography, *Son of Adam* (Andre Deutsch, 1990). Of course, I am keenly interested.

Michael Wilcox, June 1990